YOURS, MINE & OURS

ESTATE PLANNING FOR PEOPLE IN BLENDED OR STEPFAMILIES

PLANNING YOUR FUTURE SERIES

L. PAUL HOOD, JR.

© 2022 L. Paul Hood, Jr.

All rights reserved. No part of this publication in print or in electronic format may be reproduced, stored in a retrieval system, or transmitted in any form or by any means, electronic, mechanical, photocopying, recording, or otherwise without the prior written permission of the publisher.

The scanning, uploading, and distribution of this book without permission is a theft of the author's intellectual property. Thank you for your support of the author's rights.

Design and distribution by Bublish, Inc.

ISBN: 978-1-64704-465-7 (eBook)
ISBN: 978-1-64704-466-4 (paperback)
ISBN: 978-1-64704-467-1 (hardback)

This book is dedicated to you and to all who strive mightily for the "good estate planning result." I'm inspired by you. Always give them your best.

Table of Contents

Preface vii
Introduction. xv

Part 1: The Basics

Chapter 1   Working with Estate Planners. 3
Chapter 2   The Human Side of Estate Planning 20
Chapter 3   Basic Estate Planning Considerations 42
Chapter 4   Property Ownership: Means and Issues 57
Chapter 5   Types of Property 66
Chapter 6   Estate Planning Documents. 76

Part 2: Blended-Family Considerations

Chapter 7   The Estate Planning Players 95
Chapter 8   Reasons Estate Plans Fail 103

Part 3: Blended-Family Estate Planning Technique Issues

Chapter 9   Lifetime Estate Planning 121
Chapter 10 Testamentary Estate Planning. 147
Chapter 11 Putting It All Together 164
Chapter 12 Last Words of Advice 179

Appendix 185

Preface

According to research by the Williams Group,[1] the overwhelming majority of estate plans—70 percent—don't work out well for the family. Consequences may range from intrafamily litigation over the estate plan to total cutoff of relations and communication between family members. Are you in that boat?

It's inconceivable to me that most people only deal with their property in their estate plans, and thus ignore the whole legacy that each plan could leave, i.e., failure to address the impact of an estate plan on the relationships of the survivors of the decedent, often due to overfocus on so-called "tax savings." Yet, people keep doing the same type of estate planning (i.e., overfocus on tax minimization while ignoring the impact of the estate plan on the relationships of the survivors) and keep getting the same results.

The Definition of Insanity

This definition of insanity is attributed to Albert Einstein: "repeating the same action and expecting a different result." One of my goals is to reverse the patterns of failed estate plans and dysfunctional behavior that sadly too many families have repeated over generations.

---

[1] Roy O. Williams and Vic Preisser, *Preparing Heirs: Five Steps to a Successful Transition of Family Wealth and Values* (Robert Reed Publishers 2010).

The Parade of Horribles

Sadly, 70 percent of families who have experienced failed estate plans make up an inordinately high number of situations in which one partner has children that aren't the children of the other partner, i.e., so-called "blended families"—more about that term shortly.

Here are two disastrous estate plans of blended-family decedents. In the first, I had to administer the decedent's estate after the decedent's death. The second story is a case that ended up as a reported judicial decision in California.[2]

John[3] married four times (but to only three women—wives two and four were the same person) during his colorful and successful life. He had a child with his first wife. He had several active and large closely held business interests that he held in separate entities, as either the majority or sole owner. I wasn't involved in his obviously problematic estate plan.

In his will, he named his surviving spouse (wife two and four) and his daughter from his first wife as coexecutors of his estate. Unfortunately, while John was probably of the opinion that naming the coexecutors both honored and protected his daughter with his first wife and his surviving spouse, he neglected to acknowledge that his daughter and his surviving spouse didn't get along while he was alive. Yet, by naming them as coexecutors, he effectively forced them to work together. That turned into a nightmare.

Immediately following John's death, the coexecutors appointed in his will each engaged separate counsel, and they started suing each other and filing motions to remove one other. Almost weekly motion litigation between the coexecutors ensued. After nearly a whole year of roughly weekly hearings, the frustrated judge, who was supervising the administration of John's estate, removed both coexecutors, and instead, on his own motion (a very unusual move), appointed a CPA and a lawyer as successor co-administrators of John's estate.

In the California case, the husband and wife married later in life, and each had separate *grown* children. Each engaged separate counsel to represent their respective interests in their own independent estate planning.

---

[2] Sindell v. Gibson Dunn & Crutcher, 54 Cal. App. 4th 1457 (2nd Dis. 1997).

[3] Not his real name.

The husband hired a prominent national law firm to coordinate transfer of interests in closely held entity (his separate property from inheritance) to his daughters. His lawyers advised the husband to make gifts of some of his interests and then sell the rest of the entity interests to his daughters. Because the husband's property to be involved in the transaction seemed clearly to be his separate property from the inheritance, his lawyers didn't advise him to get the consent or acknowledgment of this separate property from his wife.

The wife had independent wealth of her own, and she was represented by separate counsel. Unfortunately, the wife became incapacitated. Three years after the husband's estate planning transaction with his daughters, and after his wife had become incapacitated, *her* children sued the husband (their stepfather) to nullify the husband's estate planning transactions, asserting that the property the husband transferred to his daughters was community property between the husband and the wife.

A year after the wife's children filed suit to nullify the husband's gift/sale to his daughters, on grounds that some of the transferred property was actually the incapacitated wife's community property, the husband's daughters sued their father's lawyers for malpractice for failing to get the wife's consent to and acknowledgment of the gift/sale. The trial court dismissed the husband's children's action against the husband's estate planning lawyers as premature because there hadn't been any damage yet—the lawsuit from the wife's children hadn't yet been concluded.

On appeal, the appellate court reversed, holding the matter over for trial. The appellate court reasoned that damage in form of attorney's fees to defend against the action was damage in and of itself, and the appellate court remanded the case for trial. The case never went to final judgment and probably settled.

The bottom line: estate planning for blended-family couples can be very tricky and certainly not for the faint of heart.

Why I Wrote This Book

I became acutely aware of the maddening difficulties that blended-family couples and partners had in estate planning very early in my estate planning career, which has spanned almost thirty-five years. I noticed that blended-family couples and partners faced issues that single-relationship couples and partners didn't face.

I also noticed that the estate planning community hadn't devoted as much focused study on estate planning for blended-family couples and partners. In mainstream press, there are fewer than five books on the subject, and for estate planning professionals, only a couple of books exist.

I first began studying, speaking, and writing about the unique and challenging issues in estate planning for blended-family couples and partners over twenty-five years ago. I have written articles on this subject for professional estate planning publications and have presented at meetings and conferences (as well as several webinars).

Why, you ask?

For starters, I wanted to help blended-family couples and partners. I consistently have found that blended-family couples and partners were my most challenging clients because of the emotional and legal issues that they face. Richard Barnes, who also authored a book on this subject years ago, described estate planning for blended-family couples and partners as "relationships squared." He's absolutely right. The fact that little attention had been devoted to this difficult subject significantly motivated me.

And then life happened. To me.

I got divorced and remarried and had my own blended family. Now I was *personally* facing the same gnarly issues that my blended-family clients had faced, and resolution wasn't any easier, which further motivated me to write this book.

In short, I'm one of you. I faced these issues and problems myself.

I wrote this book for *us*. I used my personal and professional estate planning experience to write a practical and helpful book that fills an inexplicable gap in guidance on the perplexing difficulties that blended-family couples and partners face. My book is effectively the second book on this subject, and the other book was written in 2009.[4]

Congratulations on Buying This Book

Congratulations! I want to acknowledge you right from the start, as your choice to open this book puts you in a special group of people who are proactively

---

[4] Richard E. Barnes, *Estate Planning for Blended Families: Providing for Your Spouse and Children in a Second Marriage* (Nolo 2009).

considering their particular family's future needs and well-being after the time of their deaths.

Even though it is well-known that there is a potential cost in not creating a formalized estate plan, the percentage of people who have their planning documents in good working order remains dramatically and frighteningly low.

According to a 2019 survey of more than 1,000 people by caring.com, only 40 percent of adult Americans have a will, even though a majority of Americans say that estate planning is important. The first significant step toward resolution of a problem is recognition and awareness that there is a problem.

Begin with the End in Mind

I am a big fan of the late Dr. Stephen Covey's *Seven Habits of Highly Effective People* and a particularly strong proponent of his second habit: *begin with the end in mind*. I firmly believe that estate planners should meet their clients exactly where they are.

With more than thirty years of experience working with family dynamics and estate planning, I've discovered some key distinctions and practices that allow you to develop your strategy and plan in conjunction with your advisors in a way that will address your particular and unique family needs and goals.

My purpose is to address the complexities that blended families face in estate planning and to allow you to be informed in a way that promotes decisions that truly work for all the members of your family, further strengthening your bonds and connections during your life and long after your passing.

My Purpose for Writing This Book

This book is not an introduction to estate planning (although I've certainly explained many of the basics). There are plenty of books that explain estate planning at varying levels of complexity. The appendix to this book contains a list of recommended books on general estate planning.

The purpose of this book is to address in detail the nuances—the mortar—of estate planning and to help you meet your goals, address your concerns, and tackle your particular issues with your estate planner. Communication is the key to good estate planning.

The Truth: The Statistics about Marriage Are Grim

It is estimated that approximately 30 percent of marriages in the US are remarriages for one or both partners. The marriage statistics for blended-family couples are grim: 60 percent of second marriages and 73 percent of third marriages end in divorce, which exceeds the 50 percent divorce rate for single-marriage couples. While we all want to enter into our first, second, or third (or more) marriages and partnerships believing we can beat the odds, these very real statistics must be taken into consideration in your estate planning.

While irrevocable lifetime estate planning (i.e., significant lifetime gifts) can be a useful tool, it is generally not recommended for most couples because of the larger possibility of splitting up. The regret and high cost of legal fees in the attempt to reverse irrevocable decisions can have a dramatic impact on the future well-being of the estate for those you want to benefit from it the most.[5]

Since this book will discuss many topics that relate to estate planning, I intend that the book be used as a reference guide for attorneys and regular folks alike. It can be read sequentially, or you can choose chapters and topics that are most relevant to your current circumstances. Estate planning is hard enough. I wanted to do my part to make it a bit easier to navigate, especially for blended-family couples and partners.

The "Bricks" and "Mortar" of Estate Planning

Since I will be considering points that can spell success or failure in an estate plan, I will not be spending much time on what I will refer to as the "bricks" of estate planning: wills, trusts, family entities, powers of attorney, charitable entities, life insurance and annuities, and living wills.

Rather, I will spend my time talking about the subtleties of estate planning that are almost never discussed but are points that can, and often do, make all the difference between a good and beneficial estate plan or a bad and unsuccessful one. In fact, I will refer to these subtleties as the "mortar" of estate planning. Let's face it—bricks without the proper mix of mortar do not build a very strong structure and will collapse under the slightest bit of stress.

---

[5] See Chapter 8 for more information about irrevocable estate planning.

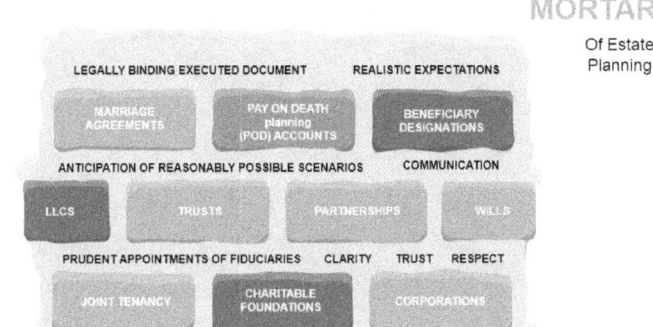

Organization of This Book

Part I focuses on the basics of estate planning. In Part II, I tackle planning issues that impact families. Part III offers observations and suggestions based on my years of experience working with blended-family estate planning technique issues.

Introduction

This introduction will define terms that you will need to know as you work through your estate planning. I will also give you some examples of blended families, which you'll see again in Chapter 11. I'll conclude this chapter with an attempt to frighten you about the perils of intestacy—particularly for the blended family—which will hopefully move you into action on your estate planning! Dying without a will and a carefully considered estate plan is especially risky, especially for blended or stepfamilies.

Definition of Estate Planning

Estate planning is a process that is ongoing until death. Estate planning is every bit as much a *process* as life itself.

You may be doing estate planning without even realizing it. For example, when you buy real estate, you are doing estate planning by how you title the property. When you buy life insurance, or get a new job and fill out the beneficiary designations for your employee benefits, you're doing estate planning. Sometimes, when you open a bank or brokerage account, you're doing estate planning as well.

Don't get distressed about the never-ending nature of the estate planning process. Since you've chosen to read this book, you're showing you know how important it is to accomplish all that you can now in your estate planning. I also know that you'll feel better when you take action and complete and sign your important documents. You're giving yourself and your family peace of mind and assurances that would not otherwise be there. It would be unfortunate, costly, and unnecessarily painful for those you leave behind if you were to die unexpectedly without an estate plan or with unsigned drafts of estate planning documents.

My purpose is to bring to light all the various sections of estate planning for blended families that you will want to consider and the ramifications of those choices. I will also show you that your documents and decisions will likely need to be updated and changed over time as your family grows and evolves so that you can have your assets and your values be fully expressed and utilized during and after your lifetime.

Remember: *Unsigned documents don't count!*

Estate planning involves more than preparing a will. Your estate plan communicates your thoughts and desires about financial management, health care, and property distributions through the drafting and execution of legal documents and beneficiary designations.

Your estate plan involves periodic review and revision to reflect the changes that you will experience throughout your lifetime, such as a new child, divorce, remarriage, loss of a loved one, or any other life-altering event. An estate plan should also be reviewed upon a major change in the law. I advise you to review your estate planning documents every year to see if your plan still outlines what you want to have happen at the time of your death.

Unless a major change has happened in your life, there is no reason to hire a professional to review the documents annually. However, I advise a professional review your estate plan about every five years to make sure you are taking full advantage of any legal changes.

Definition of Blended Family

A blended family is one in which two people are partners and at least one of the partners has one or more children who are not the birth children of the other partner.

Note that throughout this book I'll be referring to couples as "partners" and not as "spouses." The simple fact is that many people are opting, for a variety of reasons, to not get legally married nowadays yet remain together as a couple. In fact, pursuant to the most recent census, the fastest-growing segment of the population is unmarried couples.[6] Some can't legally marry, and some choose not to, yet they are together as a couple and may even have children from that relationship or other relationships. In my opinion, it would have been an oversight to leave out any type of blended family from this book.

I also believe it is important to consider two adults who are looking at mindfully approaching their last wishes and legacy planning as partners, and I treat my clients in this manner. I have seen a lot of damage done to relationships by lawyers and other advisors working with individuals by not taking into consideration the concerns of the multifaceted partnership they comprise.

Examples of Blended Families

This book focuses on the issues that arise with estate planning for blended families. Other books cover general estate planning and sophisticated methods and techniques of estate planning. They're useful to read in conjunction with this book.[7] Throughout this book, I'll discuss various estate planning techniques and how those techniques work specifically within blended-family dynamics. Let's get started by exploring various blended-family scenarios.

Blended families come in all shapes, sizes, and configurations. Perhaps the best-known blended family is the fictional Brady family, of television fame. However, today's blended families can look quite different from the one we saw on *The Brady Bunch*. Consider the following six examples of blended families:[8]

Yours, Mine, and Ours: Harry, sixty-two and divorced, marries Marge, forty-eight and divorced. Each has adult children from their prior marriages. Harry and Marge also have a minor son together. They have been married for fifteen years, and Marge stays at home to raise the child, while Harry works to support the family.

---

[6] Chanell Washington, "Unmarried Opposite-Sex Couples Living Together More Likely Than Married Couples to Both Work," referenced at https://www.census.gov/library/stories/2021/06/unmarried-opposite-sex-couples-living-together-more-likely-than-married-couples-to-both-work.html, June 9, 2021.

[7] See the Appendix for recommended titles.

[8] See Chapter 11 for more detail about each of these types of blended families.

Empty Nesters: Bill, seventy-two, is a widower with grown children and a pension, and he is the benefactor of his wife's life insurance. Bill marries Marlene, also seventy-two, who is a widow. The couple survives on Social Security, rental income from Bill's condo, and Bill's IRA.

Eat, Drink, and Remarry: John, sixty-three, marries Judith, thirty-five, as his fourth wife. John has some expensive alimony obligations to his first wife. He also has a son, thirty-seven. Judith, who has been divorced twice, has two sons, eleven and eight respectively, each with a different father, with whom she shares custody. Judith has substantially more wealth than John, while John has far greater income-earning potential as a professional. John and Judith have a separate property prenuptial agreement.

The Brady Bunch: Mike, forty, a widower, has three sons. Mike marries Carol, thirty-eight, a widow who has three daughters. They have no joint children. The children are all minors who live together. Mike owns his own business, and Carol has a substantial separate estate that she inherited from her late first husband.

May-December Relationship: Franklin, eighty, a wealthy widower with three grown children in their fifties, marries Bambi, twenty-six, an impecunious dance instructor who has a seven-year-old daughter. Franklin and Bambi would like to have a child of their own. Franklin has done a substantial amount of lifetime estate planning, and he has given significant wealth to his children and grandchildren.

Nontraditional Blended Family: Marie, forty-six, and Angela, thirty-seven, are a married couple. As a single parent, Marie adopted a child, who is now eighteen. Angela, who has been divorced once, has a ten-year-old child whom she is raising alone with only meager, sporadic child support. Marie stands to inherit money from her parents, but that may be in doubt due to her choice of partners. Angela has the greater income, and she owns the home they live in, although both are contributing to the mortgage payments.

These examples are not intended to be exhaustive. There are many other examples of blended families, all of which have valid, vital concerns when it comes to making sure the needs of loved ones are addressed in life and after death.

Even a quick consideration of each example demonstrates the diversity of blended families. In some of the examples, the couples have minor children living with them. Others do not. One couple has joint minor children. One couple wants to have a child together. In a few of the examples, the couple has children from a prior union who live part-time in their home, while other couples do not have to deal with part-time resident children. In two of the examples, the new partner is younger than the children of the other partner.

Advisors with a narrow focus of what defines family and how to protect assets may miss the various ways individuals in blended families consider all the people in their lives to be part of their family. These concerns need to be taken into account in the estate planning process.

Each of these examples also presents very different estate planning issues. In some of the examples, one partner has substantially more wealth than the other partner. If that partner dies first, should his or her entire estate be held for the surviving partner? This becomes even more complicated when considering the disparate ages of adult children from a prior marriage and minor children from the current marriage, all of whom are concerned about how the estate will pan out for them—whether they say so or not.

In other examples, one partner has substantially greater earning capacity than the other. Should that earning capacity be cut off at death, and how will the other partner be sustained financially? In one of the examples, one of the partners has very little financial experience. Who should manage her assets if she is the surviving partner? One of the couples has a prenuptial agreement—is it consistent with the couple's other estate planning documents? In another example, one partner has significant obligations to former spouses. How will the obligations be affected should that partner die first?

Simply put, there is no "one-size-fits-all" estate plan for a blended family. Every estate plan for a blended family is different, and the concerns and goals of the families are undoubtedly different as well.

The Perils of Intestacy

You don't have a will? Guess what—you still have an estate plan, even if you haven't deliberately and proactively created one yet. Do you know what it is?

What happens if you don't do any estate planning? The next few pages will scare you into doing some formalized estate planning, if perhaps nothing else will.

If you don't do any planning, your estate plan is called *intestacy* (being without or dying without a legally valid will). You might be unaware of it and its particular ramifications in blended-family situations. Under current law, intestacy tends to choose the surviving spouse as the recipient of the bulk of the property and usually puts the surviving spouse in control of the estate. This can be very challenging and potentially lead to hard feelings and possible litigation from any children of a prior union. You may have wanted your children to be considered, and you may even have made promises to them verbally. In the past, the law strongly favored children of a deceased spouse over a subsequent spouse, but this is no longer the case, even despite the increasing incidence of divorce.

In addition, if you are not married to your partner, you may receive *nothing* under the intestacy laws of your state,[9] although this appears to be changing very slowly. It is still essential for unwed partners to do their estate planning if either wants the other partner to share in his or her estate.

Medical and End-of-Life Decisions

Who will make medical decisions for you if you cannot?

As bad as intestacy is, not doing any estate planning can actually be *worse*. Suppose you're in a coma, or you have dementia; if you don't have an advanced health-care directive or power of attorney for health care (these names are interchangeable—different names are used depending on where you live), your spouse, partner, parents, or children may have to make those decisions through a court procedure called *guardianship*. This adds complexity and cost to a situation that is already emotional and painful, which could have been easily handled with an advanced health-care directive.

In a blended family, particularly one that is not close (e.g., the partners got together after the children became adults), health decisions can create a very difficult situation as your life is in the balance. For instance, your children may

---

[9]   In the United States, every state has its own laws of intestacy which can differ greatly. You can check out the intestacy laws of your state by going to www.mystatewill.com.

question your current partner's motives in making certain health-care decisions for you. It could get even worse if you aren't legally married. Your partner may have no say whatsoever; doctors might not even speak to your partner (due to patients' privacy rights concerns), and your partner may not even be allowed in your hospital room!

While disagreements could still occur with an advanced health-care directive in place, the directive states the person you wish to make the final decisions. Without an advanced health-care directive, you are doing your partner *no favors*.

Who will decide to discontinue life support if that is your wish? Again, your partner and your children may make that decision, but they could encounter difficulties if family members disagree among themselves or if the doctor or hospital balks at the decision without a court order. Cases involving these situations have gone all the way to the United States Supreme Court, which can get very expensive in both legal and medical fees—not to mention how emotionally draining and charged these issues are. If you and your partner aren't legally married, your partner, who may know what your intentions are relative to being maintained on machines, may have no legal right to make those decisions on your behalf.

Financial Decisions

Who will handle your business and financial affairs if you aren't able to do so?

Without a durable power of attorney for property management, your loved ones will be stuck with an onerous court procedure called *conservatorship*, which applies to the management of property for someone who can't manage his or her own property and hasn't appointed someone to represent him or her. Conservatorship is not only expensive, but it makes all your financial and personal information a matter of public record that anyone can access. Conservatorship can usually be avoided by having a well-drafted durable power of attorney and/or a funded living trust, the latter of which I discuss in Chapter 8.

There are things that a durable power of attorney can accomplish that probably can't be done in a conservatorship proceeding. Again, an unmarried partner may have no recourse if you become incapacitated because the incapacitated partner's children will have priority to be named conservators.

Indeed, this contingency could render the unmarried partner homeless if the conservator sells the home in which the partner is living. (I wouldn't include this grim scenario if I hadn't witnessed it firsthand.) My commitment is to educate, inform, and mitigate unnecessary pain and suffering in the face of grief and loss.

If you die without any estate planning, who receives your assets and in what proportion will depend on the type of property and its titling. Property that passes by will or by intestacy is called *probate* property. This comprises most of what people have, such as personal property, vehicles, most bank accounts, some real estate, stocks and bonds, and the like.

If your property is titled as joint tenants with rights of survivorship, the property won't need to go through probate.

However, *how* property is titled will determine whether that property is subject to probate in your state or province. If property is titled as joint tenants with rights of survivorship, the property won't go through probate but instead will pass to the surviving joint tenant, no matter what your will or trust says.

When you purchase real estate as a married couple, you're liable to get a joint-tenancy deed unless you specify that you don't want it. This is because realtors and escrow officers generally do not understand the potential ramifications in blended families related to the various methods of owning real property. It is important to note that it makes a big difference whether you live in a community-property state (where each spouse owns and has the right to give away by will an undivided one-half interest, which the owner spouse could give to someone other than the surviving spouse) or common-law jurisdiction (where spouse co-owners usually are joint tenants, which means that the surviving spouse becomes the full owner of the real estate by virtue of surviving the other spouse).

It is essential in good estate planning for your estate planner to review real estate deeds to determine how that property will pass at death. He or she also needs to know how you want to go about addressing these very important concerns.

While joint tenancy helps take care of the surviving partner, it could also impact the surviving children. The children of the first partner to die could lose out entirely on their inheritances, as the children most likely to receive assets shared in joint tenancy are the children whose parent outlives the other.

When animosity exists between partners and their stepchildren, this becomes a real concern.

Intestacy laws used to favor the children, but today, they generally favor the surviving spouse, which may seem odd given the rate, ease, and speed of divorce. Again, with very few exceptions, if you and your partner aren't legally married, the surviving, unmarried partner will generally receive nothing, even if that partner has been a partner for a long time. Probate property is generally divided between the spouse and children, although in several jurisdictions, the spouse could receive it all. Moreover, for estates that will owe federal estate tax, there can be adverse federal estate tax consequences to dying intestate, primarily through loss of the marital deduction. Intestacy is rough justice for partners in blended families; no one should die intestate.

Nonprobate Property

Nonprobate property includes life insurance, annuities, retirement plans, and US Individual Retirement Accounts (IRAs). However, it can also include pay-on-death (POD) accounts (sometimes referred to as transfer-on-death [TOD] accounts).

Most nonprobate property passes directly to the person named in a beneficiary form to receive the asset at your death. In other words, nonprobate property doesn't pass by will. Quite often, clients sign these beneficiary forms without even realizing that they are doing estate planning, especially since most people don't save copies of the beneficiary designation and almost never think through the ramifications of the beneficiary designation.

Take a minute and consider your current situation. Have you confirmed that your *former* spouse is no longer a beneficiary of your nonprobate property, which you aren't required to, and do not wish to leave to, him or her? In most areas, if you die while a former spouse is still named as a beneficiary, that former spouse will be entitled to the proceeds of the account. There is nothing that anyone can do about it, unless your former spouse willingly gives it up. Cases like this occur all the time, so take action to prevent this from happening in your situation.

Name *contingent beneficiaries* for your nonprobate property so that if your original beneficiary doesn't survive you, your nonprobate property won't pass to your estate.

One area of nonprobate property that gets frequently overlooked is backup beneficiaries, which are called contingent beneficiaries. Many people don't get around to naming contingent beneficiaries at all. These asset documents usually specify (buried in the boilerplate language of the policy or plan document) that if your beneficiary doesn't survive you, the proceeds pass to your estate. In other words, they become probate assets. As such, these assets are subject to the same intestate problems discussed earlier concerning passing, pursuant to the state or province's estate plan for you (intestacy), not your own.

If this isn't enough to get you motivated to get your documents in order, things can actually get *worse*. Usually, your creditors cannot reach nonprobate assets. However, if these assets inadvertently become subject to probate because you didn't name a contingent beneficiary, your creditors could lay claim to these assets too. If these assets are retirement plans or IRAs, income tax on the entire proceeds could be due a lot sooner than it would have had there been some thought given to contingent beneficiaries.

Obtain advice from a professional when naming beneficiaries of nonprobate property.

Although I discussed it earlier, it bears repeating: property titled as joint tenants with rights of survivorship (or as tenants by the entirety) is also nonprobate property. Again, if you want your children to get your part of that property, you better count on being the surviving partner for that to happen. Otherwise, your children will receive nothing unless the other partner, who will have no legal obligation to your children, agrees after you're dead to give them something. In estate plans that don't involve both partners and that don't take into consideration all the concerns, this very rarely happens.

Couples in blended families need to take the time to truly listen and understand each partner's motivations and concerns related to all the children in their lives. By doing so, much can be done in the estate plan so that the surviving partner is well provided for, and the wishes of how the estate could pass to the surviving children from prior relationships are met. I work with people to design scenarios and structures where there's a win-win feeling, as opposed to the more adversarial, protective, "mine versus yours" mentality that so often shows up. By keeping the mindset of "yours, mine, and ours" foremost in the conversation, new possibilities and solutions can emerge, and everyone can feel a sense of alignment.

What Makes Estate Planning for Blended Families So Hard and So Necessary?

Estate planning can be difficult even for people who have had only one partner. When people take on new partners, especially those who have children of their own, the complexities in estate planning multiply exponentially. While I know that I'm stating the obvious, it is somehow overlooked in terms of taking action: every one of us is going to die.

Many people believe that they don't have enough possessions to necessitate estate planning. However, everyone has something that someone else wants when they are gone. This could range from family keepsakes to family companies. While I use the term "blended families," I'm well aware that in many instances, your family can feel anything but blended, where there may be little or no relationship between your current partner and your children from previous relationships.

Oftentimes, one of you may be the glue that keeps the blended family together. Guess what can happen after you die? Without a plan shared in advance that honors all your loved ones, survivors often fight over virtually nothing of value. Despite the fact that many partners in blended families believe that they must make an excruciating choice between their partners and their children in their estate planning, spelling out who you want to get your belongings is far superior to doing nothing and letting them fight about it after your death. There are ways to include all of them so that there is a sense of value for the people in your life and what matters to them. This will do wonders to minimize arguments about "things."

Action Steps

Review any estate planning documents you have that are signed and legally binding. Do they reflect your current wishes and current family structure? Note any changes you see that need to be made and write down any questions that may have occurred to you by reading this section. You may be considering some of the following questions:

- Is our real estate in joint tenancy, and is this taking care of both of our most important values and concerns?

- Who are the written beneficiaries of our individual and shared non-probate properties? This includes life insurance, annuities, retirement plans and Registered Retirement Savings Plans (in Canada), IRAs (in the USA), and pay-on-death (POD) accounts. Are these the beneficiaries I want now? Do we have backup beneficiaries named?

- Determine the status of your power of attorney and durable power of attorney or advanced health-care directives. Are they in place and with the people you want to be in those roles? Are those people aware of their roles and what is required of them? Are they aware of your expressed wishes?

Put all these relevant documents in a locked, protected file and make copies for both yourself and your partner. Make sure the relevant parties in your estate plan know where these documents are located.

Create a binder with tabs for each section so that as you go about your estate planning, all the information you are gathering is easily accessible in one place for yourself and your family members should something happen to you or your partner unexpectedly.

Schedule specific appointments in your calendar for you and your partner to tackle estate planning questions and concerns. If it's scheduled, you'll take action and get it done! I recommend one to two hours bimonthly, or three to four hours once a month, during which you dedicate your focus and attention to your specific estate planning questions until you determine answers and strategies that you can implement. This will expedite your work with your attorney and accountant while also helping them do their jobs more effectively and to your satisfaction—and it will save you a great deal of money. Make it a goal to have one aspect of your estate plan decided and signed every two to three months so that you are making regular, steady progress toward your overall goals.

Most couples know how important it is to do their estate planning, and yet they tend to avoid that which is uncomfortable and that which they do not understand. Their fear of making a wrong or poor decision often causes them to not take any action at all. This causes them to make a default decision to go into intestacy, which is not a choice anyone would want to make, given the ramifications.

One coaching strategy I have seen work well for couples committed to making proactive legacy planning choices is to incorporate fun and rewards during the estate planning decision making. Some couples enjoy scheduling time on a Saturday afternoon, and then afterward going out on a date as a reward. Other couples take their notebooks and resources with them to a weekend getaway and spend time planning for their future as they also plan for what will happen after they die.

Couples who are serious, or who want to expedite this process, often hire consultants to keep them on target to make sure they are addressing that which matters most to them in ways that they would not otherwise be aware. By having committed, ongoing, scheduled meetings with a consultant, there is accountability along with an investment of time and money that helps you stay on track to get your goals achieved. Hiring a consultant for estate planning is like hiring a personal trainer for when you want to seriously get into shape!

PART I
THE BASICS

Working with Estate Planners

Introduction

This chapter concerns itself with the subject of working with estate planners. Knowing the different advisors and what their particular roles are is empowering and allows you to direct your estate planning moves. Take time to get to know these different roles and their purpose so that you best know how to move and direct each of them toward your goals.

Who Does Estate Planning?

There are many different professions who provide various estate planning and related services. Attorneys (also known as lawyers) are the only ones who can and *should* prepare the legal documents that implement an estate plan. This is because if there's a dispute over the documents, the court system will likely get involved.

Here's an extensive (but not exhaustive) list of other professionals who are important to the estate planning process:

- Accountant, Certified Public Accountant (CPA), and Chartered Accountant (CA)

- Financial planner
- Stockbroker
- Life insurance agent
- Bank trust officer
- Planned giving advisor
- Employee benefits specialist
- Asset protection specialist
- Family business consultant
- Family wealth coach

It would be wise to involve these professionals in rendering estate planning advice specific to your blended-family situation. Their professional advice can play a key role in the creation and implementation of your estate plan.

Too often, people think that wills and trusts are the only estate planning documents, but this isn't true. Beneficiary designations on life insurance policies, retirement plans, and Individual Retirement Accounts (IRAs) can be much more important than traditional estate planning documents if they transfer more wealth than a will or trust, which is the case for many people.

Additionally, pay attention to how property is titled, especially real estate and bank accounts. As I have discussed previously, property that is titled in joint tenancy or pay-on-death passes to the survivor when the first joint tenant dies, irrespective of what your will says, so it really is an estate planning document. Most people don't realize that they are essentially doing estate planning when they buy a piece of real estate, get a job, buy life insurance, or even open a bank account.

Where Do You Find Estate Planners?

Where to find estate planners is one of the most difficult questions to answer. There are so many different professions that offer estate planning advice. Perhaps the best way to find estate planners is by word of mouth. Nothing speaks louder than a satisfied client. However, word of mouth is not always reliable.

You want estate planners who have significant experience; this is *not* a task for amateurs or those who only dabble in estate planning. Some jurisdictions permit specialization of lawyers in estate planning. Additionally, the American College of Trust and Estate Counsel (ACTEC), which is a premiere trusts and estates attorney organization, maintains a list of its fellows on its website.[10] However, there are many qualified estate planning attorneys outside of ACTEC. Another helpful attorney organization is WealthCounsel,[11] a membership organization for lawyers that provides their lawyer members with up-to-date estate planning forms, practice management advice, marketing, and networking.

In the United States, an organization that helps find all sorts of estate planners (i.e., both attorneys and nonattorneys) is the National Association of Estate Planners & Councils,[12] which gives a designation to qualifying individuals called Accredited Estate Planner®.

When sorting through all the possibilities, a good qualifying question to ask up front is whether the person has experience with the complexities of blended-family estate planning. If the person says that he or she does, ask for specific instances and listen to how he or she describes not only the makeup of the client's family, but also the way that he or she approaches handling the particular situations that a blended family needs addressed. After reading this book, you'll have a list of questions you can ask. When asking those questions, see how the person responds. Is this something the person is familiar with? Is it something he or she would recommend? This initial interview can help indicate how well the person will work with you and will also allow you to direct the process. You can also ask if he or she has clients with blended families who would be willing to talk with you so that you can directly hear about their experiences.

Who Should Be on Your Estate Planning Team?

Though everyone's situation is different, there is a simple answer to this question. You need as many estate planning team members as it takes to get the job done. Most people will only need an estate planning attorney, although that attorney should coordinate efforts with the client's other advisors (e.g., accountant, investment advisor, life insurance agent).

---

[10] www.actec.org.
[11] www.wealthcounsel.com.
[12] www.naepc.org.

Sometimes, there will be situations where one of your advisors may recommend bringing in another advisor to assist you. Seriously consider doing as they suggest because it is important that you get your estate planning done correctly. This is particularly important in blended families, as it is my experience that clients often get stuck in the estate planning process due to the complexity of their unique planning needs.

How Do Estate Planners Charge for Their Services?

The fee estate planners charge for their services will vary depending on the type of estate planning advisor. Most estate planning attorneys typically charge by the hour, although there will be some attorneys who charge a flat fee for some estate planning services. The problem with blended-family estate planning is that so many factors, such as the fee, often depends on the family involved.

In my experience, estate plans for blended families often cost more than other estate plans because of the additional complexity that blended families require. Don't let this stop you—estate planning is important for you and your family. I believe that the money spent on the front end saves a lot of money in the long run, as problems are addressed and minimized or eliminated altogether. An experienced estate planning attorney should be able to give you a range of expenses to anticipate. However, you should understand that if your situation is unusually complex, that range may widen.

Other estate planning advisors take fees in a variety of ways, from hourly to commission-based to a percentage of assets under management. You should always be told upfront how the advisor will charge and when he or she will expect payment.

The more prework you do, the more efficient your advisors' work, and the more likely it will yield the results you want.

How Do Estate Planning Attorneys Do Their Work?

There are two ways that an attorney may represent a couple—and this is critical to the blended family. The first way is to represent them jointly, which means that either partner can't keep secrets from the other. If one partner asks the attorney to withhold some information from the other partner (e.g., a proposed change to a document), the attorney's only option is to withdraw from representing both of you.

Secrets and differences of opinion tend to occur more often in blended-family situations, so if you know in advance that you want to do something in your estate planning that your partner won't like (e.g., put his or her interests in trust with a third-party trustee or favor your own children instead), you may want to give serious consideration to being represented by separate estate planning attorneys.

Research has shown that 70 percent of estate plans where secrets are kept and plans are made that impact whether someone has a say in the matter tend to fail.[13] This typically comes from a lack of communication and trust in the family system. Nothing invites litigation more quickly than having something imposed on you from the grave.

The second way that an attorney can represent a couple is to represent each separately. In this situation, the attorney simply treats each partner as a separate client. This may sound strange, especially if the two partners are seeing the attorney together. However, this would permit the attorney to withhold information from one partner. The attorney must be very careful in this situation not to favor one over the other. If a conflict arises between a couple, the attorney would have to withdraw from representing both parties. This method is not very common, and there is some controversy among attorneys as to the efficacy and ethics of this arrangement. Nevertheless, many attorneys believe that separate representation is ethically possible (in states and provinces where this is allowed by law).

I've never represented a couple separately, and it hasn't come up that often where there was a need to do so. In other words, there are either clear signs that separate representation of only one partner is the necessary route, or there are signs that joint representation is possible. I note, however, that an attorney often only represents one partner in a blended-family relationship because the partner who hired them wanted it to be that way.

---

[13] If you want to know more about this research, see *Preparing Heirs* by Roy Williams and Vic Preisser.

The Initial Interview

Introduction

The formal estate planning process really begins with the initial client interview by the estate planner. This initial interview is critical. The estate planning process can come to a screeching halt if the initial interview goes badly. There is no way to predict how an initial client interview will go; each interview is a creative act that can change in an instant, shifting from great to terrible with just one wrong comment or look. This is because estate planners are simultaneously trying to obtain the relevant facts and engender or bolster confidence in themselves while attempting to establish rapport. It's quite the dance for all involved.

To aid in this process, I've come up with a list of questions that both clients and planners may be thinking during the initial interview. The following question lists were designed after interviewing both clients and estate planners and contain virtually every thought I've ever heard from both the client and estate planner during the initial client interview. You can use these question lists to tap into what resonates with you and what concerns you have. Review question lists 1-1 and 1-2 prior to meeting with potential advisors and highlight the ones that jump out at you and your partner.

Question List 1-1: Questions a Client May Secretly Have during an Initial Interview with an Estate Planner

- Can this person help me (or us)?
- Will I be able to work with this person?
- Am I physically safe with this person?
- Does this person make me feel uncomfortable?
- Is this person going to offend any of my loved ones or hurt anyone's feelings?
- Is this person going to be loyal to me?
- Will this person take the time to talk *with* me, not *down* to me?
- Can this person explain issues and considerations clearly to me and my family?
- Does this person understand that some of these decisions are going to be very trying?

- Will this person be perceptive enough to understand what I do not or cannot express clearly or directly? Will this person even make an effort in this regard?
- Will this person respect my feelings and desires and not try to take over to save me taxes?
- What is really in it for this person?
- What is this going to cost me?
- Is this person going to take advantage of me either on a fee or work basis?
- How long will this take?
- Will this person be timely and prompt?
- Can I call this person whenever I want? If not, when may I call this person?
- May I call this person at home? On weekends? After hours?
- Will this person return my calls in a timely fashion? Are our definitions of "timely" the same?
- Will this person keep my affairs confidential?
- Will this person give me his or her undivided attention during our meetings? Will this person take phone calls or office interruptions while we are meeting?
- Where will I fall into this person's work priorities?
- Will this person meet me at my home or another location, or will he or she meet only at his or her office?
- If we eat a meal together, will this person charge me for the time we are eating?
- How will this person handle "soft office costs" (e.g., copies, faxes, long-distance charges)?
- Will I talk to this person only, or will I have to deal with other employees in the firm? If so, who else will I have to deal with?
- Does this person have a "gatekeeper" (i.e., someone to go through first to talk to him or her, such as a personal assistant)?

For clients in blended families, the additional thoughts are often foremost on their mind:

- Does this person understand the unique situation of my blended family?
- Does this person have experience with blended-family scenarios like mine?

- Does this person have any judgments or biases when it comes to blended-family issues and choices?
- Does this person have personal experience with blended-family issues, such as a divorce and/or stepchildren, which may cause him or her to project and not remain objective?
- Can this person effectively help me sort key decisions?
- Does this person understand what I'm up against regarding the conflicting needs of different members of my family?

Question List 1-2: Questions the Estate Planner Is Wondering about the Client during the Initial Interview

- Am I physically safe with this client?
- Does this person make me uncomfortable?
- If meeting with more than one person, either scheduled or unscheduled, is it too many people with which to meet?
- Is the client mentally stable? Or at least stable enough to execute legally valid documents or enter into legally binding agreements?
- Is this client able to pay reasonable fees for me to do the estate planning work that I feel he or she needs?
- Will this client pay reasonable fees for the work that I perform?
- How much handholding will this client expect or require? Does this client understand that this can have a bearing on fees or desirability to have him or her as a client?
- Will I run into a complication that will cause the final cost of my services to be significantly higher than the quoted fee (or fee range)?
- Can I rely on this client's representation of the facts and figures? How much "due diligence" will I have to do?
- Can I fit this client into a standard form or plan that I have developed with minimal "original thought of drafting" (meaning, without additional risk-taking or cost)? Will this client understand this reality, or should I go over that now and possibly alarm the client needlessly?
- What are this client's expectations regarding turnaround time and my personal availability?

- Will this client permit me to allow his or her work, or at least the first drafts, to be prepared by the person in my office most competent to perform the work at the lowest pay scale?
- With whom may I speak while doing this work? With whom should I absolutely not speak?
- What confidentiality issues are present with this client? Should I send mail, faxes, or electronic correspondence to a particular address? Should I call prior to sending? May I leave voicemail messages to say that I called?
- Will I enjoy working with this client?
- Will I regret that I ever agreed to take on this client at the quoted rates?
- Will I encounter problems with the client's spouse, children, or significant others?
- How clear must I be that I do not represent or work for anyone but the client?
- Will this client want me to work with his or her spouse or partner as well, and is this something I will be able to do?
- Will this client ask or pressure me to do anything that would compromise my personal integrity or even my professional license or designation (e.g., backdating documents, misleading others about document's effects, forging signatures, not following formal execution procedures, lying or omitting material health information on a life insurance application)?
- Am I being used as part of this person's agenda other than estate planning?
- Is it likely that this client, or his or her family, will sue me or attempt to drag me into a fight after the client's death or during a divorce on an involuntary, nonpaying basis as a witness?
- Will this client be pleased with my work or with the work of *any* advisor?
- How many other advisors has the client gone through before me? Why?
- Will this client present problems that I lack the confidence or competence to handle?
- Would the client allow me to bring in help? Should I discuss this candidly up front, or will this needlessly alert the client that he or she should choose another advisor?
- Will this client work with me in conjunction with the rest of his or her estate planning team, and give me permission to coordinate with others so that our efforts are all in alignment?

- Can I expand my services with this client into other needs, including those of companies owned by the client?
- Is it likely that this client will refer me to other friends or relatives?

Realities of Estate Planning

It is very important that you feel that the estate planner is truly listening to your goals and concerns and not simply collecting facts to plug you into a prefabricated estate plan. Unfortunately, this happens a lot. If you sense that the estate planner is not really listening to you, you need to hire another estate planner.

It doesn't matter, the estate planner's reputation. Estate planners are human too, and they have good and bad days. They get on well with some people but don't connect with others. A true professional will certainly understand your decision to move on so early in the process.

If you go through more than one estate planner, be careful that you aren't setting yourself up for failure by unintentionally sabotaging the relationship at the outset. Perhaps you aren't ready to delve into estate planning. If both partners in a blended family can't agree on an estate planner, consider hiring separate estate planners.

The act of "shopping" for the "right" estate planner should only go so far. If it goes on too long or involves consideration and rejection of several estate planners, it may mean that either you or your partner is simply looking for an estate planner who will agree with him or her, which can indicate an ulterior motive. It could also indicate that either you or your partner may have unresolved issues related to initiating the estate planning process., such as mortality salience (fear of discussing death). Don't let these fears, motives, or issues keep you from your goal. If your partner is not on board, you may want to consider practicing communication strategies to get to the heart of the matter and move forward together with ease and grace. Or it may mean that you need to proceed alone without your partner on your personal estate planning, because, all other things being equal, it's better to get your estate process underway and completed rather than staying stuck because the two of you can't get on the same page for whatever reason.

In my experience, I have found that estate planners who ask clients "good questions," i.e., pointed questions about your estate planning goals and concerns, tend to have far better luck getting the necessary information over estate planners who simply ask clients to complete questionnaires or overtalk to demonstrate the estate planner's estate planning knowledge and expertise.

At my initial client interviews, I listen to my clients, as I firmly believe that my clients are there to talk about their situation and not to hear me pontificate on how smart I am or what, theoretically, could be done first. After my clients provide information about their goals and concerns, I often allow at least thirty to forty-five seconds of silence, often uncomfortable silence, to pass.

Why? It's to make my clients realize that I'm expecting more information, and the client now understands it's safe to give that additional information, which usually ends up being more important than the information provided in the initial answer. It's like peeling an onion. Then I ask more questions. Every client is different; some clients need more prompting than others, while some need help focusing on the most pertinent estate planning issues.

The initial interview in the blended-family context presents more opportunities for problems than virtually any other initial client interview. Whether they want to openly admit it or not, the blended-family couple usually has divergent interests, particularly when at least one of them has children from a prior union. That typically comes out in the initial interview if people are being candid, but this does not always happen. One partner might want to make sure that his or her children don't get cut out of his or her inheritance, while the other partner may only be worried about what he or she will get from the other (i.e., security).

I have seen numerous initial client interviews involving couples in blended-family situations end quickly after each party's true intentions were stated. When possible, a referral to a wealth coach was necessary to help the couple sort their differences in the best way possible. An initial interview that goes badly can trigger a lot of hurt, misunderstandings, fears, and resentments. Having a place to bring these emotional land mines while working with a professional who can help navigate the fallout will make a huge difference in the overall estate planning process, and more importantly, in the couple's relationship as a whole.

In instances where a couple is unable to sort out their differences and where their goals continue to diverge, a valid and viable option is to have separate estate planners representing each of their individual interests. I still maintain that having clear communication with each other throughout this process will go a long way toward keeping the family out of courtroom battles after death.

Showing Up to the Initial Interview Prepared

During the initial interview, the estate planner will ask for a lot of information. The checklist below contains a list of documents that an estate planner will probably need, although this list can vary from estate planner to estate planner. When in doubt, ask the estate planner why he or she needs that particular information. I can assure you that the information listed in this checklist is necessary to do a proper job.

Checklist: Information the Estate Planner Will Need

- [ ] Copies of all prenuptial, postnuptial, and property agreements with your partner and former partners
- [ ] Copies of all property settlements and all divorce decrees from former partners
- [ ] Copies of marriage contracts with current and former spouses
- [ ] Copies of all life insurance policies and beneficiary designations
- [ ] Copies of the beneficiary designations for all retirement plans and accounts
- [ ] Copies of all real estate deeds
- [ ] Copies of all gift tax returns filed
- [ ] Copies of the most recent brokerage and bank statements
- [ ] Copies of employment-related agreements (e.g., employment contracts, deferred compensation agreements, stock options)
- [ ] Copies of current estate planning documents (e.g., wills, living trusts, powers of attorney including property and health care, living wills)
- [ ] Copies of all trusts in which you are a beneficiary or trustee
- [ ] Copies of all closely held entities (e.g., limited liability company, corporation, partnership), articles of incorporation, bylaws, operating agreements, shareholder agreements, and buy-sell agreements for all businesses in which you have an interest
- [ ] Names and contact information of all of your children, stepchildren, and any other person to whom you wish to give a share of your estate
- [ ] Copies of any other estate planning documents that are presently in place
- [ ] Names of primary advisors with a request for permission to talk to them

- [ ] Copies of current financial statements of assets and liabilities.
- [ ] Copies of income tax returns for last two years
- [ ] Copies of any charitable pledge agreements
- [ ] Information on all bank and savings accounts (i.e., in whose name each account is titled and method of title, as well as joint tenants, tenants-in-common, or pay on death)
- [ ] Information of persons (e.g., children or elderly parents) you are either obligated to support or are currently supporting
- [ ] Information on your estate planning goals
- [ ] Anything else that is relevant to your particular blended-family situation: _____

While this checklist may feel overwhelming, it can help break down the task of preparing for estate planning into small, easy steps. Choose one box at a time and see how much information you can organize in fifteen-minute chunks of time.

What Is Too Much Information?

Some clients balk at providing so much personal and financial information to an estate planner who, in many cases, will be a total stranger. There are valid reasons why the estate planner is asking for that information; many of them should be obvious by reading this book. Your estate planning advisors need this information to provide you with their best efforts and to not make mistakes. You should either give them everything that they ask for or find another estate planner to whom you are willing to entrust such information. It is *that* vital.

Some clients purposely exclude very important information because they feel that it is too sensitive or not relevant to estate planning. This happens a lot more when a blended-family couple shows up together for estate planning. Some couples haven't developed the trust necessary to give each other this information. Sure, there may have been property disclosures if the couple entered into a prenuptial agreement prior to marriage, but this often isn't the entire picture. Lots of significant personal information, such as private wealth and other assets, are often withheld.

Given that only 20 percent of couples who remarry talk about finances prior to the wedding,[14] withholding information is likely to be the case. Understandably, someone entering a second (or third or fourth) committed relationship is likely to be more wary if his or her first trusted union ended in a contentious divorce. This may signal a lack of trust the divorced person may unconsciously have in himself or herself to adequately choose lifelong partnerships that are trusting and lasting.

I once had a client who brazenly told him that he wouldn't give the entire picture to any of his professional advisors, only giving each person the information he felt they needed. In this way, the client said that he felt safer and more in control of his situation—no one advisor knew everything. This strategy backfired on him when a mistake was made that I could have easily caught if I had known all the facts. In my opinion, this "strategy" is a big mistake, and in my experience, it is probably the number one reason why an estate plan either fails or isn't implemented properly.

There are ways for clients to remain in charge of their estate planning process without resorting to hiding information. One of the biggest areas clients misrepresent is the value of their estates. In my experience, people lowball their net worth or leave out a significant part of their property, especially after a certain net worth threshold. This is ill-advised, to say the very least.

Take a minute to consider the likelihood that you will withhold or misrepresent information when speaking with your advisors. I know that many of you will. I've conducted informal polls during presentations where I asked the audience if they had ever not told the entire story of their financial life to a professional advisor. Almost every time, roughly two-thirds of the audience sheepishly raised their hands.

If you withhold or misrepresent your financial position, you could receive the wrong estate plan structure—especially if you understate it. The estate planner may have recommended a different estate planning technique had you accurately stated your financial position.

In blended-family initial client interviews, personal facts are often dismissed for the sake of the union. For example, perhaps the couple don't agree

---

[14] C. B. Burgoyne, and V. Morison, "Money in Remarriage: Keeping Things Simple—And Separate." *The Sociological Review*. 1997;45(3):363–395, at p. 365, which reports the results from a 1989 study by Marilyn Coleman and Lawrence H. Ganong of the University of Missouri.

on the role that the surviving partner will play in administering the deceased partner's estate or trust as executor or trustee—it's not unusual for a partner to insist on being in sole control of his or her partner's estate or trust, which the other partner either doesn't want or wants to include his or her children. It's also not unusual for partners to disagree over whether the partner's children will receive anything from the parent partner at death. If the partners know that they won't agree on a particular point, they simply try to avoid it. These issues often are too raw for the parties to successfully address and work out.

It is not unusual for the parties to seek the assistance of a counselor or coach who is trained to address communication problems when information feels too fragile to share. Very few estate planners are trained to help in this way. I encourage you to seek the support you need to move forward openly and respectfully, seizing this opportunity to strengthen and further deepen your relationship as a couple and perhaps even with your children.

If, after attempting to use professional support, you find that you still lack the ability to openly discuss potentially contentious and contradictory concerns, I strongly recommend separate representation of partners. This is because an effective estate plan requires that you have complete candor and honesty with your advisors.

One final note: When working with estate planners, it is important to let them know your expectations of their time. Some estate planners are slow; others might move too quickly. You should let them know the speed at which you'd like to proceed. Be aware that they will expect you to show up at the pace you set. This book is designed to support you in being as prepared and ready as you can be to draft your blended-family estate plan efficiently and expediently.

Action Steps

Get two three-ring binders and some clear plastic sleeves to store your documents. You will both want your own binder so that you each have access to all the needed information, especially if you will be working with separate attorneys.

Once you're ready to begin, you'll each need three different highlighters. This is so that you can highlight each item on the checklist as you get them together. One strategy that works well is to use different colors to track your progress. For example, you could highlight in yellow the first one on the list you will address so that it stands out. Starting with the easy items is a great idea so that you get a sense of accomplishment right away!

Mark in your calendar when you will put that particular item in the binders. Once you take an action toward getting that documentation in your hands, you will highlight the same one, let's say in orange, so that you know it is in progress. When you have put that particular set of documents or information into the binder, highlight that same line with pink, for example, so that in an instant you can see that was completed.

I recommend doing a little victory acknowledgment of some sort when you've completed one task. People come up with great ideas for this, such as a bite of a favorite chocolate or drinking a nice cup of tea. You'll be much more motivated to keep going if your little wins along the way are acknowledged, even if only by you. You could also show your partner the win, and then look at the list together and see which one you will do next. Perhaps each of you can take on different tasks to divvy the work and make it go that much more quickly. You'd then highlight in yellow the next one and start tracking your progress all over again.

My clients often express how this makes the process easier and more enjoyable, as they see the baby steps along the way. The more pleasurable you can make the experience the better! Many clients also report that they enjoy seeing the checklist become more colorful as they move toward completion. I recommend planning something special together after the entire checklist is completed and your notebooks are ready to go (e.g., going to dinner or some other favorite date-night experience). This is not fun work, but it is very important, so it's great to reward yourselves all along the way!

The Good and Bad Signs When Choosing an Estate Planner

The Good Signs

- Estate planner listens before talking.
- Estate planner asks "good" (pertinent, direct questions about your goals and concerns) questions.
- Estate planner focuses more attention on family issues than tax benefits/results.

- You have a good feeling about the estate planner.

The Bad Signs

- Estate planner does all of the talking.
- Estate planner doesn't listen to you.
- Estate planner puts more emphasis on tax efficiency/benefits.
- Your gut doesn't feel good about the estate planner.

The Human Side of Estate Planning

Introduction

All estate planners and clients should be united in their search for and implementation of a *good estate planning result*. What is that, you ask? In my opinion, a *good estate planning result* is one in which those you want to leave your possessions to get them the way you want and when you want, with taxes minimized and relationships after death enhanced or at least not negatively affected. The taxes and property transmission are easy (or relatively so). It's the relationships piece that can be elusive.

A Good Estate Planning Result

Recall that in the preface, I laid out a model that distinguished between the so-called "*bricks of estate planning*," i.e., wills, trusts, beneficiary designations, etc., and the "*mortar of estate planning*," which includes realistic expectations of the inheritors, communication, trust and respect, etc. A solid estate plan requires *bricks* to be held together by the right mix of *mortar*.

Back to the "*good estate planning result.*" The truth is that the path to a good estate planning result can be very difficult. To illustrate the difficulty of this trip, I developed the following graphic model, which I call the *Path of Most Resistance?*© (Path).

The Path

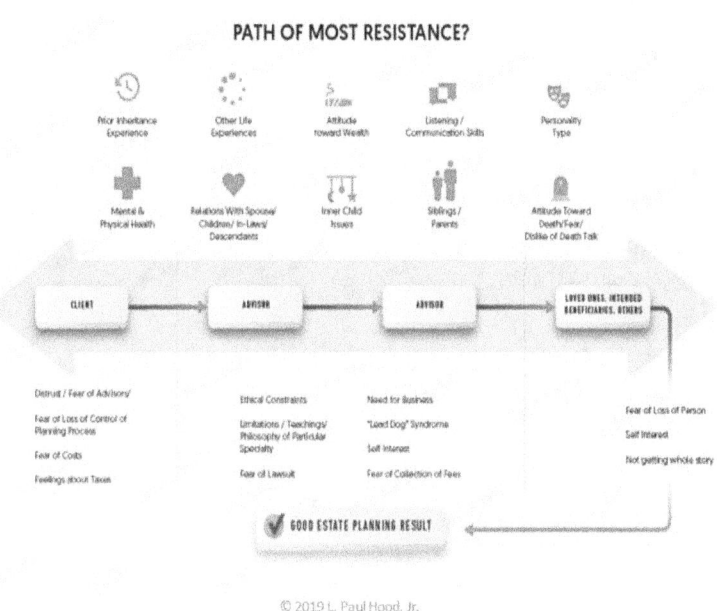

In the Path, the factors above the line are factors with which heirs, estate planners, and folks such as yourself have to deal. Factors below the line are characteristics that you, your estate planning advisors, and your heirs may possess. As the Path illustrates, there are several "players" in the estate planning "play."

The matters above the thick double arrow represent views and common experiences among all of the "players," and the items below the double arrow are witnessed in each of the respective various players in the "play."

This book will assist you in achieving a *good estate planning result*, which, as you will discover, is usually more challenging for a blended family than a traditional family. Sometimes, the best you can do is to not surprise anyone by the results of your estate planning.

Key Elements of a Successful Estate Plan

There are three key elements of a good estate plan that must work in unison for the plan to even have a chance. The following Sweet Spot graphic best describes this relationship.

The Three Elements of Good Estate Planning

Every estate planning tool or technique used must carefully match the *players* (you and your family usually), the *assets and cash flow* used in the tool or technique, and the *tool or technique itself.* In my experience, virtually every failed estate plan contains at least one mismatch between the players, assets, and the technique.

The Sweet Spot

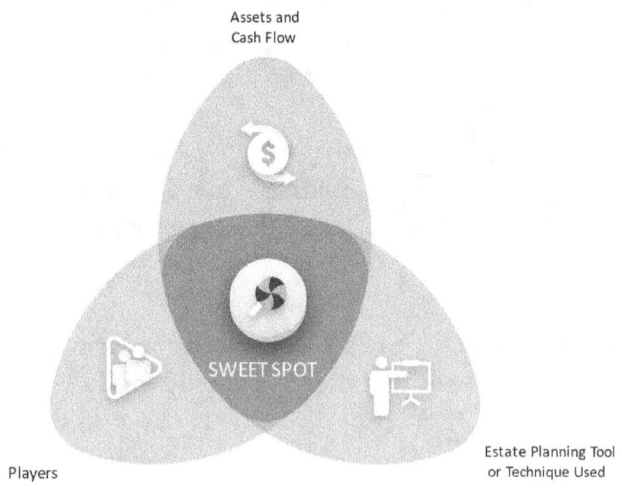

© 2020 L. Paul Hood, Jr.

Common Fears Associated with Estate Planning

I have concluded through my years of experience that estate and will planning are not favorite activities for very many people. In a radio commercial, famed broadcaster Charles Osgood once said that, for him, estate planning ranked right up there with *root canals*! Why is that?

Although the statistics range a bit, it is estimated that 50 to 70 percent of Americans die without a will or without having done any deliberate planning. At an intellectual level, all rational human beings know that they are going to die eventually. So why not plan for death? While there are myriad reasons why people avoid taking the necessary actions related to sound estate planning, most of them relate to fear and pain avoidance. People tend to avoid that which is painful or uncomfortable, no matter how important it might be for them to do it.

What part of estate planning makes you the most uncomfortable? Whatever it is, don't let it stop you!

Twelve Fears Involved in Estate Planning

What are people afraid of? I have identified twelve of the most prevalent fears that I've encountered when it comes to estate planning, all of which are valid and real:

1. *Fear of contemplating death:*

While everyone knows they will die eventually, many people are uncomfortable thinking about their own deaths or the death of their spouse or partner.

Most estate planners think that fear of death is the main reason that their clients procrastinate in their estate planning. Many mask this fear of death with a feeling that "it isn't my time" or "I've got more time," which is somewhat irrational because no one knows their time of death in advance.

However, I believe that this procrastination issue is much more complex than a fear of death alone. The additional fears that I have identified also contribute as much or more to the procrastination or failure to act when it comes to estate planning.

2. Fear of not doing the right thing:

Some people are so afraid that they might make a mistake in their estate planning that they won't even begin to plan. What many people don't realize is that their state has an estate plan for them, called intestacy, if they die without a will. Whether consciously, or from denial or avoidance, intestacy often is a much bigger mistake than any plan a person could make on his or her own. To learn more about the pitfalls of intestacy, review the section entitled "The Perils of Intestacy" in the introduction.

3. Fear of the unknown:

Estate planning requires some projection of future events. Some clients are so fearful of what the future may bring that they put their heads in the sand and simply do nothing with respect to their estate planning. This fear has a ring of irony to it, as the result of failing to plan is certain—the estate reverts to intestacy.

4. Fear of hurting someone's feelings:

The fear of hurting a loved one's feelings has caused many clients to procrastinate in their estate planning. For example, a parent may be fearful of hurting the oldest child's feelings because the parent believes it best to select the youngest child as successor trustee or as successor president of the family business. This fear becomes even more pronounced in blended-family estate planning, where a partner may perceive estate planning as having to choose between his or her partner or his or her own children. This fear is one that robs people of being able to take effective actions that they know are in the best interests of all their family members. From an attorney's perspective, it is also irrational because the estate plan won't function well if you pick the wrong person or if you don't choose anyone at all.

The irony of avoidance continues if you enter intestacy, as intestacy grants certain persons priority to handle certain jobs, such as an executor, and these persons may not be who you envisioned for such positions. This can be particularly difficult for blended families, where there may be certain members of the family who would not be honored or acknowledged by intestacy who you would have very much liked to have included. When the law takes over the administration of an estate, the subtle nuances and dynamics between family members, ones that you know well while you are alive, are not taken into consideration. The unfortunate result is that a blended family is more likely to become estranged upon the death of a parent.

5. Fear of estate planners:

People often fear even the professionals they have selected to help them. The knowledge gap between estate planners and clients really bothers many clients. For example, a person who is not accustomed to being in a lawyer's office often is uncomfortable being there, even for his or her own estate planning. Many clients feel distrustful of lawyers and resent the costs associated with estate planning. When these emotions impact a person's ability to work collaboratively with his or her legal and estate planning team, there is often a much greater emotional and sometimes financial cost to the family at the time of the client's death.

The time of death is already emotionally charged with the loss and grief of the loved one. Chaos and confusion are added to this situation if there is no understood and agreed-upon plan in place.

A good estate planner should be able to estimate in advance a range of costs for most estate plans. With this book in hand, you can learn how to work effectively and efficiently with your advisors to maximize their time and minimize the monetary costs.

6. Fear of the estate planning process:

Some people freeze when it comes to planning their own estates. In that Charles Osgood commercial example, he associated estate planning with root canals, even though there is not one bit of physical pain involved in estate planning. The same people who can jump right in and make suggestions for other people's estate planning simply can't do it for themselves. I've come to suspect that the reason for this is that clients fear losing control of the process to the attorney or to someone else along the way.

I fondly remember a client who carried around drafts of estate planning documents in a briefcase for almost ten years. I ran into the client in an airport five years later, and he showed them to me, almost expecting my praise for still having them. I firmly believe that this guy was convinced that concluding his estate plan meant that he was going to die shortly thereafter and that by postponing execution of the documents, he was somehow cheating death. In fact, completing your estate planning will ease stress and bring peace of mind that will improve the quality and length of your life.

7. Fear of running out of money or losing security:

This fear is often associated with suggestions made by estate planners that the client engage in some sizable lifetime gift-giving or enter into a significant estate planning technique. As life expectancy has risen in the past century and continues to increase, the fear of outliving one's assets has grown exponentially as well, especially with the looming specter of a loss or reduction in social security and potentially high medical costs toward the end of life.

Some people attempt to justify putting off all their estate planning based on this fear alone. This fear is irrational when used for this purpose because lifetime irrevocable estate planning is but a small part of the estate planning process. Indeed, where blended families are concerned, estate planning may not involve any irrevocable lifetime estate planning strategies, as the odds make this a less-than-wise choice in most circumstances.

8. Fear of law changes:

Some clients simply procrastinate because they are so fearful that the laws may change after they sign their estate planning documents, which would result in having to revisit their estate planning. This stems from the erroneous belief that once an estate plan and will are completed, the process is over and done. The reality is that the estate plan you make now is for life as you know it *now*, with the understanding that as you continue to live, your wishes and your estate will continue to evolve, requiring you to revisit your estate planning documents and make changes where necessary and desired.

I encourage people to embrace change as a part of life and to incorporate change as part of their planning strategy. This often puts their minds and hearts at ease, as they realize they don't have to figure out every single possible scenario the first time around. There is freedom to address unanticipated events as they become aware of them and figure out what to do about them.

People are reassured when they learn that most estate planning documents are revocable and amendable. In my experience, the unsettled nature of the federal estate tax for approximately the last thirty years has caused many clients to put off their estate planning, and I've seen some terrible situations where well-intentioned people die without a good plan and leave a mess for their blended families.

9. Fear of facing reality:

While they may not fear estate planners or death, many people simply don't want to face the reality of the importance of tending to their estate planning. The reality is that the law provides an estate plan (i.e., intestacy) for those who don't come up with their own, so this fear is irrational. People who don't want to face reality will nevertheless be subjected to it, or worse, their families will.

For couples in blended-family situations who are not married, relying on the default intestate plan option is really not an option at all, as your partner will not be acknowledged or honored in the way you may want him or her to be. The law is focused on the legalities of situations and relationships, not on the level of care and commitment. Check out your state's laws on common-law unions and intestacy to get a sense of that reality.

For couples in blended families who are married, you also need to consider your plans related to the stepchildren in your lives, or any birth children you may have. For partners who have been involved in the lives of their stepchildren and step-grandchildren, taking the time to specify how you would like them to receive your various assets would be a very wise and prudent way to proceed. If you do not declare what you want to happen in legal terms, it will likely not happen (or if it does, it may not happen as you would have hoped).

10. Fear of loss of flexibility:

Some clients don't want to engage in any significant irrevocable lifetime estate planning for fear of the loss of flexibility relative to their future. Knowledge and understanding go a long way toward alleviating this ungrounded fear. Irrevocable lifetime estate planning options are something that you can read about in this book and others to see if they are viable options for you. With so many options to choose from, and with estate tax laws changing frequently, there are pros and cons to using irrevocable lifetime estate planning options. I am not a strong advocate of these options in blended-family situations, and I will go into greater detail regarding each option in Chapter 8.

11. Fear of loss of privacy:

Some people won't begin any deliberate estate planning because they are reluctant to divulge personal and financial information to an estate planning advisor or possibly to their partners. I've seen many situations in which clients conceal relevant asset information out of fear that someone else would learn about their financial situations. I have navigated several blended-family situations where trust in the family needed to be rebuilt before people were willing to be open about all the details of their estate with one another. The need to keep things hidden is a detriment to effective estate planning, as prudence dictates that all relevant information be given for the estate planner to prepare the most optimal estate plan.

I've seen some people attempt to hide behind false or incomplete information, such as an understatement of their own wealth, as a justification for not going forward with a suggested estate plan, even when it would be in their blended family's best interest. This self-defeating behavior stems from a belief that it is better to hide and keep some things secret than to have an open and honest approach to how they want life to look for their loved ones after their death. What I continue to find odd about this is that the specific details will all be known after death, and the degree of regret and resentment the remaining family members will encounter can take an extraordinary toll on their well-being and quality of life.

12. Fear of probate:

The fear of *probate* wasn't part of the original eleven fears associated with estate planning, but I subsequently added the fear of probate after personally witnessing someone express such palpable fear of probate that it prevented forward progress on a proposed estate plan draft. When I encounter someone who exhibits a fear around probate, the first thing that I do is define what probate means and to explore exactly what probate does.

The term "probate" comes from the Latin word *probatio*, which literally means "to prove." This term refers to a judicial proceeding where the court first reviews, approves, and accepts the decedent's last will and testament as valid, followed by the judicial process of giving legal effect to and implementing the decedent's last will and testament. However, the term "probate" today refers to the *entire estate administration process* and not just to the will-proving piece, and this is how most people define probate.

Interestingly, the proper court gets involved in administering a decedent's estate even if the decedent dies without a valid last will and testament for the purpose of recognizing the legal heirs of the decedent who are entitled to succeed to the decedent's property pursuant to applicable state laws of intestacy. Even though there's no last will and testament in intestacy, the judicial proceeding of intestacy often also is called "probate."

Simply put, the overall purpose of probate laws is to lay out an orderly process whereby the property of a decedent is transferred after death pursuant to applicable state laws of descent and distribution, i.e., either pursuant to a last will and testament or pursuant to applicable state laws of intestacy. The probate process protects against mayhem and self-help occurring when someone dies. Moreover, the probate process protects the rights of the decedent's valid creditors. There are some estates that are so contested or problematic that need careful judicial supervision

Many years ago, it was commonplace for probate laws to be very procedural and involving significant, hands-on court supervision at every step of the process. Probate also tended to create many opportunities for judicial appointments in connection with the probate process, which greatly increased the cost of the probate process, and because the heavily regulated judicial proceeding took extra time, lengthy delays became commonplace.

Beginning in the 1960s, there was public backlash against inflexible state law probate systems and the associated costs and time delays. Nonlawyer Norman Dacey wrote a very popular revolutionary book, *How to Avoid Probate*, that was very critical of probate laws and systems. It suggested use of funded revocable trusts, joint tenancy with rights of survivorship, pay-on-death accounts, and beneficiary designations as testamentary substitutes to avoid probate. Mr. Dacey's tome was very popular and created quite a stir.

In response to the popular uprising concerning antiquated probate laws, state legislatures began streamlining probate laws. Within a fairly short period of time, much of the unnecessary procedural delays and appointments had been eliminated in just about every state, with one notable exception: California, where I advise people to structure their estate plans to purposely avoid probate. Subsequently, most states have now adopted an informal, out-of-court estate administration option called *independent administration*.

In many cases, the fear of probate was based on horror stories about "probates from Hell." Unfortunately, these stories are isolated occurrences and don't reflect the usual experience. For starters, many probate horror stories are very old vestiges of times during which state probate laws were much more rigid and inflexible.

Today, probate laws are not a significant problem. When someone expresses fear of or antipathy toward probate, it's invariably due to a lack of current information about probate. In my experience, after I explain the information about probate, the person gets over the fear.

What Do These Fears of Estate Planning Cause?

These fears prevent people from doing estate planning or cause them to procrastinate in their estate planning. Fears lead to avoidance strategies that cause delays in estate planning. I have seen many an estate plan come to a screeching halt when children do not want to discuss life after their parents' death. The parents simply decide to put off estate planning rather than make their children uncomfortable, which is almost always a mistake. Never mind the fact that their children may either dislike or not be ready to handle what happens with intestacy. The "child" may likely be an adult with children of his or her own, with his or her own estate planning needs to consider, which makes knowing his or her parent's plans that much more important.

When children are dealing with divorced parents who both have different plans based on the shared assets with new spouses or partners, the children involved are even more in need of sound advice and guidance on how to best address the desires, goals, and concerns of their parents.

Often, people tend to avoid those conversations due to a lack of awareness about how to have the conversations effectively. Children in blended families often feel that what they want or care about doesn't really matter. Often, they refrain from speaking about their concerns out of fear of being perceived as entitled or greedy—when all they really want to know is what they can expect so that they can do sound planning for themselves. Knowing how to have these conversations makes a huge difference for the entire family. This is especially true when certain family members will have key roles to play in the estate plan, such as executor or trustee. Make sure your executor and trustee are prepared for their roles.

You Are the Sum of Your Life Experiences

I love the quote: "Wherever you go, there you are." Give it some thought, and you'll likely agree. All I have seen, heard, and done in the past has a major bearing on my current likes, dislikes, feelings, and opinions.

So, where have you been?

Where do you fall in the birth order in your family of origin? Birth order can play a significant role in how people perceive certain aspects of estate planning. Historically, it has not been that long since the oldest male heir took on the entire estate under the ancient doctrine of *primogeniture*. Today, birth order still subtly impacts estate planning through the frequent default use of the oldest child as executor or successor trustee. If you're the oldest child, this might suit you just fine, and you might see no problem with this plan. However, if you're not the oldest child, and you think you're better suited as an executor or trustee, your view of selecting the oldest child as successor may be quite different. Perhaps you had an experience with an older sibling where that sibling was favored solely because of being older, and you resented it.

For example, if you're the only daughter in a family of brothers, you may find yourself as the primary caregiver your parents turn to for assistance and help. They may rely on you more than your brothers but still give the oldest brother the responsibility of carrying out their wishes. This can be confusing when you may know and understand their wishes better than your sibling.

These are important dynamics to consider as you begin to wonder which of your children and stepchildren you see in various roles related to your estate plan. Knowing how to include them effectively in the conversation can be very helpful, as well as shed light on what the various members of the next generation care about and what roles they would be open to considering.

Two variations of the Golden Rule come to mind here:

- *Do unto others as you would have them do unto you.* Take time to think about how you would have liked to be treated by your parents when it came to their estate planning and how you'd like that to translate into your estate plans.
- *Do unto others as they would have you do unto them.* What works for you might not work at all for some of your children or stepchildren. Discussing what matters to them and what they would prefer is a great way to honor them as you move forward and can go a long way

toward having the family remain connected and unified. This takes a great deal of skill and practice if you haven't opened these sorts of conversations before.

What Constitutes Being Wealthy to You?

In James E. Hughes, Jr.'s book, *Family Wealth*, he describes a family's wealth as "its human capital and its intellectual capital, secondarily of its financial capital."

Do you see yourself as wealthy? What are some of the stories and beliefs you have around the term "wealth"? Some people have clearly defined wealth parameters. Others don't. Some people are ill at ease with the thought of being considered wealthy and do not want to be defined as such. It has been my experience that people who aren't comfortable with a definition of "wealthy" rarely do any substantial irrevocable lifetime gifting, even if estate planning advisors think that gifting is a great idea and that there's more than enough liquidity[15] to do so without adversely impacting the overall robust nature of the estate.

How did you obtain your wealth? This sometimes gives clues about how you view wealth and how you want it divided. It is not unusual for people who have inherited wealth to view that wealth differently than those who made the wealth themselves. People who made their own wealth often identify themselves by their owned property. In my experience, they more often demand to retain control of their property and are more willing to take estate planning risks. They also tend to feel more confident in the realm of estate planning and in learning about all their various options.

Contrast this with the person who inherits significant wealth. With inheritors, I see two approaches most often: (1) Those who view themselves as mere stewards of the property. They usually play it more safely. (2) Those who feel that the money is theirs to do with as they choose. Often, they seem to be more irresponsible and freer with their wealth and less able to see themselves in the role of managing, growing, and furthering that wealth for future generations.

This is an unfortunate circumstance for those inheritors who were not given the opportunity or training to be competent with their finances. They often feel a great deal of shame and embarrassment around their lack of acumen with their wealth, and these emotions keep them from seeking and accessing

---

[15] How quickly and cheaply an asset can be converted into cash.

professional training, coaching, and advising that could allow them to truly flourish in their lives and build their wealth with competence and confidence. This often leads to the "shirtsleeves to shirtsleeves in three generations"[16] adage that is so common. A lack of preparedness from the inheritors is one cause for the assets and wealth being gone in short order.

Your Union

How many previous partners have you had? How many previous unions has your current partner had? Estate planning can be impacted by the number of times that a person marries or takes on new partners. Fears, doubts, and even cynicism about whether a relationship will last can creep in and impact the degree of trust you have in yourself and your partner to go the distance this time around.

Estate planning options vary in part by the quality of the current relationship. This is where I find working together as a collaborative team to be very helpful for blended families seeking sound estate planning advice. The more safety there is to honestly share the reality of your current situation, and not just the positive (or negative) imaginations you may have about your relationship, the more grounded and effective your estate plan will be for both of you.

I find that it is imperative that the two of you, as a couple, be candid with your estate planner about your relationship. For example, if the couple's relationship seems rocky, the estate planner may be less inclined to recommend significant lifetime estate planning. I once had a couple hire me to create a family limited partnership.[17] I didn't find out until after the plan had been implemented that they'd been legally separated for several years and each partner had been dating other people. Had I known this pertinent information at the time the couple came to see me, I might have given more appropriate advice or designed the partnership differently.

I used to make it a point to ask direct and indirect questions about what my clients hoped to accomplish. Questions I used to weave into the conversation include:

---

[16] E.g., the inability of grandchildren to manage the wealth passed down to them from their grandparents and parents.

[17] A holding company owned by two or more family members.

- Why do you think this is the best and right solution for your needs or problem?
- What have you considered, if at all, should something happen to your union?
- Have you considered using other options, such as a Grantor Retained Annuity Trust (GRAT)[18] or sales to intentionally defective grantor trusts, as each can accomplish the same end goal while not having the same degree of expense and challenge, in the event that the relationship ends in divorce rather than death?

Consider how well you communicate with your partner. Knowing how to communicate your emotions, hopes, dreams, and desires with each other will allow you to be much more fluid and fruitful in your estate planning process with your advisors. In addition, the quality and frequency of communication between the two of you can significantly impact the estate planning advice you're given. This is even more important in a blended family. People usually come into new relationships with their own way of doing things and often with their own property, as well as standing legal agreements from the dissolution of prior relationships. If you don't communicate often or very well, you will generally be better served if you are represented by separate estate planners.

Health Issues

How's your health? Health issues are significant in estate planning, as some people are more motivated to act on their estate planning after beset with health issues. A diagnosis is often a potent wake-up call to get started when planning has previously been avoided. Unfortunately, once a diagnosis happens, it is often too late to take advantage of some vital estate planning opportunities, sometimes because of mental incapacity or perhaps because some estate planning techniques require some certainty in life expectancy. Sometimes people also are motivated to initiate their own estate planning by the loss or sudden illness of a friend or an acquaintance.

---

[18] A Grantor Retained Annuity Trust (GRAT) is a creature of United States tax law. In a GRAT, one creates a specially designed trust with property and retains a right to an annuity from the trust for a specified period.

Historical life expectancy in someone's family of origin can impact what advice an estate planner gives regarding possible estate planning techniques. Families who have their genome done in order to track hereditary issues should also bring this information to their estate planning advisors for better awareness of how to best design their particular plan.

Finances

Have you ever been involved with bankruptcy or been sued for a significant amount of money? Do you owe on any promissory notes, or do you have money loaned out to others? Do you have debts that your partner is not aware of that will impact them at the time of your death? Are you aware of how to protect your partner and your family members from debts and loans you may be liable for at the time of your death?

Past experiences with financial issues such as a filing for personal bankruptcy, having to defend against a large lawsuit, or being saddled with debts, give people a certain impression of their ability to properly estate plan.

Knowing the reality of your financial situation will be imperative for your advisors as they go about modeling your various options. You don't want them wasting their time and your money coming up with plans that would not apply to your current situation and obligations. You want your estate plan to be focused on what will make the most sense for you and your family.

Knowing that only 20 percent of people discuss financial matters before they remarry,[19] I am aware that your partner may not be fully apprised of all your financial details. Review what you may not have fully disclosed and consider how you might open the door to a more authentic conversation about your shared finances in the event of one and then the other's deaths.

What Will Your Family Look Like at Your Death?

Have you ever envisioned your family at the time of your death? Does the idea of discussing your family after your death make you feel uncomfortable? These and many other questions should be faced because they can provide insight as to how things will play out, including how people will react at that time. In a

---

[19] See the article cited in footnote 14, which referenced a 1989 study by Lawrence H. Ganong and Marilyn Coleman of the University of Missouri.

blended family, this can be critical because relationships usually change after death—relations between your current partner and your children may be fine during your lifetime but can shift dramatically after you're gone.

Your children, who may be cordial and pleasant while you are alive, may ignore or become hostile toward your partner, and perhaps even their half-siblings. The fear of these scenarios becoming reality often keep people from addressing the underlying issues and concerns during their life, which, more likely than not, results in that which they fear coming to fruition.

Brought into public awareness through Dr. Richard Warshak's book *Divorce Poison*, "parental alienation" is a form of emotional child abuse where a custodial parent belittles or vilifies the other parent in front of the child. When parental alienation occurs, your birth children may turn against you through manipulation by your former spouse. You may find your ability for a unified family dramatically impacted, which may influence you and how you look at your estate planning options.

For instance, birth children who think that they are entitled to a percentage of your estate may end up being written out of your will as a way of you getting back at them for their alienation. This is the saddest and most painful way people approach estate planning—as a tool to communicate pain, hurt, resentment, and anger.

I've also seen the reverse, where a conversation about estate planning can open a relationship that had been previously estranged, where important healing and reestablishment of trust can happen, using an approach aimed at responsibility, accountability, apologies, and amends. The overarching and long-lasting impact of parental alienation can be averted and reversed with a commitment to coaching toward a commonly shared goal. For better or worse, when there's an estate at stake, it can bring players to the table in ways that nothing else will.

Knowing how to have uncomfortable conversations about death and dying can be very helpful when addressing estate planning questions and ideas. People rarely, if ever, face these questions, often because other family members are more uncomfortable discussing these issues than the person hypothetically dying. Don't take what your family members share with you personally. The more you can listen from a place of knowing that they are revealing themselves and what matters to them, the more you can be present for their concerns, even as you are sorting your own obligations.

I have seen estate planning interrupted by the objections of children who did not want anything to do with a parent's death or the aftermath on the grounds that it was morbid or too far into the future to worry about. I've also seen the next generation balk at opening these conversations out of fear of repercussions. They have learned to keep their thoughts to themselves because their parents may have reacted angrily or with judgment in the past when children expressed particular desires.

With a blended family, I always advise the couple to seriously contemplate that family relationships may go south or end after the death of one partner. I wish it wasn't the case, but I've seen it happen far too often. I err on the side of realism over idealism. When you consider the statistic that 70 percent of families end up disconnected after the deaths of both of their parents,[20] it's likely that number will be even greater with the added complexity in blended-family situations.

Your Views on Life

Where did your views on life come from? Whether I want to admit it or not, we often obtain our views on life from our parents. This includes our views on estate planning. Consider your formative experiences related to your parents' choices. Also consider how your choices may have impacted your own children. Obviously, in blended families, I am including situations where one partner is not the parent of some or all of the children.

Since we experience much of our lives with our parents, there is often a fear of a parent remarrying, whether through divorce or death of one parent. Many children disagree with their parent's decision to remarry or to take on a new partner, particularly after the death of the other parent. If the other parent is deceased, some children view a parent's remarriage as somehow disloyal to the memory of the deceased parent, almost as if the surviving parent must remain in mourning forever. Their own conflicting feelings around loyalty to their deceased parent can create a barrier to engaging with their stepparent in an authentically loving and connected manner. In many instances, adult children can view new partners or stepparents as interlopers to their inheritance.[21]

---

[20] From *Preparing Heirs* by Roy Williams and Vic Preisser.
[21] For a detailed discourse on how adult children can feel about their stepparents, read the book *Step Wars* by Grace Gabe and Jean Lipman-Blumen.

Did your parents discuss their estate planning with you? Children whose parents did not discuss estate planning with them generally are far more likely not to discuss their estate planning with their own children. Some parents "discuss" their estate planning by telling their children and stepchildren various aspects of what they will be doing, even if this information changes, conflicts, or leaves out pertinent information that the parent might have told someone else. I have found that many parents do not discuss estate planning with a child until that child is also a parent. In my experience, the best estate planning includes input from all who are concerned, especially if everyone feels a sense of safety and freedom to openly share their thoughts and desires.

Sharing information can be very important when it comes to family businesses because parents will usually look to the children to take over. If the parents don't have frank and open discussions with children and stepchildren in this situation, they risk miscommunication and the children perhaps selling the business after the parents die, even though this is not what the parents would have wanted.

Sometimes it is a matter of two ships passing in the night. I recall a situation where a father lived cash poor for many years because of expensive premiums for his life insurance policy. The policy was to be used to redeem his shares in his family business, thereby passing control to his son, who also worked in the business, so the son could keep working in the business. The father told me that had his son expressed no interest in working for the business, he would have sold it and never bought the insurance. The father was undergoing some lean times all so that his son could keep the business going.

When the father died, the son immediately took the life insurance proceeds and then sold the company. The son related to me that he had hated the business and that he had never wanted to work there. However, he felt obligated to his father to do so out of a sense of loyalty. When I asked him if he had ever expressed those sentiments to his father, he said he had not because that would have demonstrated disloyalty to his family.

This was a very sad situation because if the father and son had such a discussion, the father could have lived more comfortably. Dad also could have sold the company during his lifetime for a lot more that what the son received in the sale. This illustrates costly scenarios that occur far too often due to a lack of open, effective communication related to significant estate decisions that impact loved ones during life and after death.

Past Experiences with Estates or Trusts

What past experiences do you have with estates or trusts? Our experiences with prior estates and trusts often inform our views on our own estate planning, particularly if it involved our own parents. I once had a man break down in tears in my office over the fact that his parents only left him half as much as they left his siblings. He wondered if his parents only loved him half as much. This gentleman was significantly wealthier than his parents, so it was not an issue of money—it was about love. This was a situation where the parents could have saved their son a lifetime of worry and shame by simply telling him that they were giving more wealth to their other children because they knew that he did not need it but that they loved him just as much.

Nevertheless, this same gentleman was about to do the same to one of his own children in his own estate plan by giving that child, also very successful, less than his other children. He was not going to tell that child that he loved him or her all the same until I pointed out that he was repeating what his parents did to him. Once he saw it, he changed his mind.

Children are often upset by what can simply be effective estate tax planning (where estate tax exists) by their parents, where the parents "skip" them and leave significant wealth to their children's children (i.e., the parents' grandchildren). It's not that the children are opposed to their parents saving them estate taxes. It's that the children want to have their cake (i.e., the estate tax benefits) and eat it too (i.e., enjoy the property). In other words, the children either want to have control over what their children receive or direct access to the wealth itself for personal reasons. Again, what the children want more than anything is to be included in the planning so that they are aware and understand the basis for decisions being made. This goes a long way toward averting resentment and pain that often looks like entitlement and greed.

I have found it somewhat curious that people often want things in their estate plans that differ from their views on estate plans of others. For example, I have asked clients if they believe that trusts should last forever, and they say no, yet they want this result in their own estate plans. Other issues include whether co-trustees can work together or at what ages trusts should be distributed to children. Many times, their views in general differ significantly from what they want in their own plans. Other issues that clients view differently are whether institutional trustees are desirable, whether estate plans should reward or punish certain behaviors, and how much authority or discretion should be given to trustees.[22]

All in all, the human side of estate planning plays a huge role in the process. The more your advisors have an honest, reality-based understanding of your family situation, the more your estate plan will be able to reflect your values and intentions and produce the best results for your family with regard to taxes and asset allocation.

Action Steps

First, take a personal inventory of each of the items below:

- health
- relationship to wealth and assets
- relationship with your partner
- relationship with your children and stepchildren
- relationship to estate planning

Which of these stand out as a fear? Which ones keep you from taking action? If you find yourself avoiding taking action here, stop right now and list your "what ifs" by answering the following questions:

- What if I don't take any action? What's likely to happen?
- What if I put this off and wait for another time? What's likely to happen?
- What if I take one small action step right now? What could happen? What small step can I take now toward my goal of having a healthy estate plan for myself and my family?
- What's another step I could take? What if I took that next step?

If you find yourself feeling motivated, you could write out a list of the different steps you could take now that you see as most important. By breaking

---

[22] Note: If these topics cause you some concern, or overwhelm you completely with the jargon, as you utilize this book you will become more familiar with these terms so that you can understand how they apply to your family.

down a big looming goal such as estate planning into small, bite-sized chunks, you'll have a greater likelihood of acting sooner and an even greater likelihood of completing all the actions toward your goals. Think about the tortoise—slow and steady wins the race!

Basic Estate Planning Considerations

Introduction

Estate planning is a *process*, not an event, so you should always seek professional guidance when doing it. When I was in practice, I had to fix way too many "do-it-yourself" estate plans that cost *more* to fix than they would have to create from scratch. Even though you should get professional help, you and you alone must oversee the estate planning process. This will require some work on your part, principally in reading documents and asking questions. My intention in writing this book is to empower you to feel competent and able to take charge and be the director of your estate planning process.

If you are intimidated by legalese or by estate planners, you can stay in control of the estate planning process by knowing what you want to accomplish and by requiring your estate planner to explain it to your satisfaction. If your estate planner either can't or won't explain your estate plan to your satisfaction, then it is time to hire another estate planner.

The best estate plans that I have ever been associated with involved hands-on clients who took an *active role* in the creation of their estate plan and who remained in control of the estate planning process. I was always bothered by hands-off clients who basically abdicated their estate plans to me. Remember that the estate plan is yours, and not anyone else's. To execute a successful estate plan, you need to be engaged and in control.

Your Estate Planning Goals

The first step in the estate planning process is to identify what you want to do—your estate planning goals. This step often befuddles people, and they almost always ask: What do other people in our situation do? It isn't that easy. Every family is different, especially blended families.

To help you along, I've included a list of possible estate planning goals for you to consider, many in the context of a blended family. These potential goals are not in any order. Many of these goals can actually *conflict* with one another. You won't have all these goals, either. You may even have a goal that is not discussed here. These goals are simply to give you an idea of the possibilities you can consider.

1. Retain control over assets and business decisions

First and foremost, most people want to retain control over their lives and their property as long as they possibly can. They want to decide who will be in control when they are no longer capable or no longer want to do so. The goal of retaining control is a particularly important one in estate planning for the blended family because there may be divergent interests (e.g., children from a prior marriage and a current partner) in who should get that job. Therefore, a carefully thought-out durable power of attorney, provisions for backup trustees for those who use revocable living trusts, and advanced health-care directives are a must, and even more so in the blended family.[23]

If you own a business, you may want to pay very close attention to your corporate documents to see what they provide regarding succession in office. Have the documents reviewed and coordinated with your estate plan. Failure to coordinate business documents with estate planning documents can ruin or negatively affect the estate plan.

For example, if you are being paid a salary by your own company and you become disabled, will your salary continue to be paid, and, if so, for how long? Who will make that determination? Who will succeed you in your office if you are unable to serve? Will it be a child of yours, who may be averse to his or her stepparent? Can the new person in charge fire someone in your family,

---

[23] Details about these aspects of your estate planning will be covered in Chapter 5.

such as a child? These and others are all very critical questions to which you need to know the answers to prior to disability or death.

2. Provide support for children and the surviving partner

Providing support for children and the surviving partner is not as easy to achieve in a blended family for many reasons, not the least of which are possible conflicts between children, stepchildren, and the surviving partner. Many people have a goal of wanting to provide support for either a set period of time or through an endeavor, such as the education of a minor child. Providing support to someone in a blended family can conflict with other estate planning goals, such as leaving other children an inheritance.

For instance, you might want to provide lifetime support to your partner (who may be depending on it), even if it means that your own children must take a backseat and possibly get nothing from you. There are no easy answers here. That's why you've really got to give this goal some serious thought.

Sometimes, conflicts arise between older children, for whom you provided an education, and younger children, whose education may not have even started yet. This is often compounded in the blended-family situation because the younger children might be with your current partner, whereas your older children may be from a prior relationship. You may feel obligated to support the children from your first union, even though your partner might also need (and expect) support. This situation would clearly present a conflict. However, do not allow these potential or actual conflicts to halt your estate planning; remember, intestacy or an incomplete estate plan is far worse.

3. Protect loved ones from predators and themselves

Loved ones who are young or vulnerable may need protection to ensure that their inheritance stays intact and is not reached by creditors or those who would unduly influence them and rob them of their money. In addition, with the high divorce rate, spendthrift trusts[24] may help otherwise capable loved ones from the ravages of a divorcing spouse even if they may not otherwise require trust protection.

---

[24] A clause added to a trust that is intended to protect the beneficiaries from their creditors.

In a blended family, this goal could be even more important because of the polarization that frequently occurs in these families after the death of a parent/partner. Some children are too young or immature to handle responsibility or money. There may also be a child with a disability who requires management of that child's property. Other instances, such as a drug or alcohol addiction or financial problems, can suggest the possible need for financial management via a trust.

4. Keep certain property in the family

Some families own property that has been in the family for a long time, and others own businesses that they wish to keep in the family. This requires special planning and can involve buy-sell agreements[25] or cotenancy arrangements, the latter of which can provide a method of sharing property use, revenues, and expenses.

Some estate planning goals may have to be changed to keep property in the family rather than it being sold. This is particularly true when estate or capital gains tax will be owed. In the context of a blended family, this type of property, more often than not, consists of antiques or heirlooms that have been in a family a long time. I've seen litigation occur over family heirlooms and family pictures, especially in blended families.

Sometimes, it is more important in a blended family to specifically provide who will receive the "emotional assets" (e.g., grandma's silver)—which often have more sentimental value than actual value—than it is to provide for the financial assets. People do fight each other in court over very little, and this is much more common in blended families.

5. Protect your assets from creditors, lawsuits, and undue influence

Many people don't consider asset protection to be an estate planning goal, and discussing asset protection is beyond the scope of this book. However, the litigious nature of our society today demands that we consider insuring against many of life's risks. Life insurance is important, as is property and casualty insurance, including umbrella coverage. You should consider insuring against

---

[25] Discussed in Chapter 4.

insurable losses (there is no such thing as lawsuit insurance) by using corporations or limited liability companies, or, in some cases, trusts.

In blended families, the risk of undue influence, most notably from the other parent of the stepchildren involved, is even greater than in other families. Trusts can protect against changes by others in favor of themselves late in life that would have never done otherwise.

6. Avoid probate

This may or may not be a goal, depending on where you reside. The probate process in most jurisdictions is generally streamlined and easy, but there are jurisdictions, such as California, where probate is costly and complex. In fact, in the context of a blended family, I frequently recommend that a client let his or her estate would go through probate because of the supervision that a judge would give.

I know that this seems like radical advice, but it is not. There are many situations that require oversight by someone, and we prefer that person be a judge rather than an interested family member who may not have the other member's best interests at heart. Do your research and find the arguments for and against probate in your particular jurisdiction.

7. Maintain flexibility

One goal you may have is to be certain your estate plan is flexible enough to work in changed circumstances, such as changes to tax laws or even family changes. We really don't know what the future will bring. For example, will there be a federal estate tax in the United States in the future?

Sometimes, our desire to retain flexibility outweighs all other estate planning considerations, particularly with lifetime gifting, which often makes sense in estate planning. Good estate planning documents build in as much flexibility as possible to anticipate reasonably foreseeable events. In a blended-family situation, perhaps the couple is planning on having children of their own, which may prime other goals.[26]

---

[26] The use of a trust protector can be very beneficial, and I'll briefly discuss this concept in Chapter 7.

8. Retain access to capital

This is no doubt one of the most important goals for clients that unfortunately many estate planners neglect to consider, as estate planners often overfocus on estate tax reduction. Gifting in any form, whether outright or in trust, causes the loss of access to the capital represented by the gifted property. Many people cannot really afford to part with access to capital, even though they may have a taxable estate. If retaining access to your capital is one of your goals, make sure that your estate planner knows that at the beginning. This will save time, narrow your options, and usually save money.

9. Make lifetime gifts

Another goal may be that you want to enjoy the satisfaction of seeing family members and others enjoy gifts during your lifetime. The unfortunate thing about transfers at death is that the giver is not around to see the receiver enjoy the property. People who like to see that can make significant gifts during their lifetime. In blended families, the desire to make lifetime gifts can cause conflict because someone (e.g., your partner or one of your children, to whom a gift was not made) may be very unhappy that a gift was made for fear that this might be to his or her detriment.

10. Transfer future appreciation

Maybe you have property that is expected to appreciate in value, and you'd like to get that property out of your estate before it appreciates. There are some very effective estate planning techniques that can accomplish this, such as Grantor Retained Annuity Trusts (GRATs) or installment sales.[27] In a technique called an "installment sale to an intentionally defective grantor trust," a parent can sell property to an irrevocable trust in exchange for a promissory note that calls for installment payments.

---

[27] Both are discussed in Chapter 8.

11. Transfer an opportunity

Opportunities for wealth, such as an idea for a new business or a piece of property, often present themselves to us. For some, they may consider transferring that opportunity to a loved one before the opportunity is taken themselves, which keeps the value out of their estate and therefore, the estate plan.

12. Move property to grandchildren or more remote descendants

Some clients believe that their children are well-provided for, so they are more concerned with benefiting their grandchildren. Some like to make significant transfers to grandchildren or great-grandchildren. In blended families, consider how you want to coordinate this, as you may have a variety of grandchildren with separate needs from each of your prior relationships.

13. Defer estate or income tax

Most clients' goals are to defer estate tax or income tax for as long as possible. This often doesn't make much sense when it comes to the estate tax, but many people like to do so anyway because they lack the liquid cash to pay estate tax at the first partner's death. However, many people see this as a problem for their surviving loved ones. Income tax deferral usually makes sense unless you are deferring income into periods where the tax rate will be higher. Income tax deferral most often comes into play in the setting of beneficiary designations and distribution options for retirement plans and Individual Retirement Accounts (IRAs). There are ways to stretch out receipt of benefits from retirement plans and IRAs to maximize the income tax deferral.

14. Avoid estate tax

A goal of most clients is to avoid as much estate tax as possible. In the United States, the tax law provides very few breaks from the estate tax. One of those breaks, though, is the special use valuation break. However, this is a very complex provision and only applies to estates that have a heavy concentration of certain types of real estate (e.g., farms and closely held business property). Sometimes, it makes sense to plan to retain that benefit by continuing that use, as opposed to doing something else with the property, such as selling or leasing it.

There is also a break that can be found by paying estate tax in installments (typically, it is due nine months after death). This break only applies to estates that have a heavy concentration of closely held business interests or real estate. Often, people lack the cash to pay their estate tax if they died today. Sometimes, it makes sense to plan your estate in a way so that you retain the eligibility to pay the estate tax in installments. Of course, when the federal estate tax applicable exclusion amount is high, very few people have to worry about the United States federal estate tax.

15. Avoid or minimize gift tax

For clients who wish to make lifetime gifts, one goal is generally to pay as little gift tax as possible while making the greatest amount of gifts. The United States gift tax contains several handy breaks that the federal estate tax does not have. One of them is the exclusion of tax for gifts of up to $15,000[28] to an unlimited number of people, who don't even have to be related to you. Another is the unlimited exclusion for transfers made directly to health-care providers or schools for someone else; this allows grandparents to pay for their grandchildren's tuition. It often makes sense for people to use these breaks.

There are other breaks, too. The big one though is the applicable exclusion amount for gifts made during lifetime. You can use this exclusion during your lifetime or at death, though there are possibly more benefits to using it during your lifetime if you can afford it. The biggest advantage to lifetime use is that all the income and growth in value of the gifted property is out of your estate. This is also the downside: you no longer have that property in case you need it later in life.

16. Maximize usage of United States estate tax exclusions

It often makes sense to fully use the lifetime gift tax applicable exclusion amount, which can be used either during your lifetime or at death. Use of the

---

[28] As of 2021.

applicable exclusion amount usually is a goal for most people once they are aware that it can keep their estates from being subject to the estate tax.[29]

17. Donate to favorite charities

Some people have an estate planning goal to make significant transfers to their favorite charities. There are estate planning techniques such as charitable gift annuities and charitable remainder trusts that assist in facilitating charitable pursuits.[30]

18. Achieve tax predictability or finality

If you are risk averse, it is important to discuss tax predictability and finality with your estate planner at the outset. Some estate planning techniques are riskier than others. Risk-averse people may not be interested in estate planning techniques that create any form of risk of running afoul of the taxman. This is similar to a risk assessment that you would do for investments. It is important at the beginning of the estate planning process to tell your estate planner your risk sensitivity. Of course, some people want the most aggressive estate plan they can get, and these are also available.

19. Provide tax-deferred diversification

Many people's estates hold a significant part of their value in only one or two assets (e.g., a family home or business). This is called an *undiversified* estate, which is much riskier because all the estate's money is in one investment. As the lesson in *Aesop's Fables* says, it is dangerous to put all of one's eggs in one basket. The major obstacle for those who want to diversify is the capital gains tax. There are estate planning techniques, such as the charitable remainder trust, that permit diversification of assets without having to pay the capital gains tax up front. In other words, you can keep a significant part of the tax working for you.

---

[29] You can learn more about gift tax exclusions in the United States in Chapter 8.
[30] Discussed more in Chapter 8.

20. Provide guidance and management for your children

A major goal of estate planning for many is to set up a system to protect loved ones from themselves when they are young or financially challenged. Or, perhaps one wants to give them a soft landing by doling out the money in smaller portions. Trusts and some other estate planning techniques can do a very good job of this. For example, instead of a child receiving all his or her inheritance at once, a trust can be set up to pay out the inheritance in stages or, perhaps better yet, hold the assets in the trust for life, allowing access to the assets while maintaining creditor protection of the trust assets.

21. Encourage or discourage certain behaviors

Many clients do not wish to reward their children for relying on a possible inheritance, for not obtaining honest work, or for engaging in unsavory or illegal activity. State laws (which vary from state to state) permit people to give additional money or income to their loved ones during lifetime or by will for certain types of productive behavior, such as working in a socially useful but undercompensated field like law enforcement or the nonprofit sector.

State laws, within limits, also may permit delaying or withholding an inheritance to discourage certain types of behavior, such as not working, marrying outside of the family faith (although this one often doesn't work), or substance abuse. This doesn't matter to most people, but to those to whom it matters, it seems to matter a lot.

I almost always counsel against the use of these clauses because, in my opinion, they are inflexible and there are much better alternatives, including a wholly discretionary trust, to achieve the same result.

22. Level the playing field

In many families, beneficiaries will have extremely different needs, so many clients wish to provide appropriately for those beneficiaries while not excluding the others. Estate plans should identify those who could be vulnerable after the death of a parent or partner and take steps to anticipate and minimize this vulnerability.

Leveling the playing field can be crucial in a blended family. For example, a dad decides that his second wife will have voting control over a family business by virtue of being trustee. Dad's eldest son from his first marriage, who works for the business, is then subject to the potential whims of his stepmother and could even be fired from his job with the family company. I have seen this happen.

There are ways to ensure that this either doesn't happen or is made so difficult or costly that it is unlikely. Sometimes, if it is decided that a bank or other institutional trustee will be used instead, if gives the trust beneficiaries (or a trust protector) the power to change institutional trustees and make a trustee more responsive to his or her needs.[31]

23. Provide a mechanism for resolution of disputes

Even among family members who get along during life, disputes may (and generally do) arise after the death of a parent. Providing a mechanism for resolution of disputes can be critical in estates in which a fight is possible or even expected. A system for either arbitrating or mediating disputes should always be considered in estate planning documents for a blended family, as court fights in blended families are far more likely than in other families.

24. Keep certain assets away from certain people

Some clients know that certain beneficiaries would not handle the inheritance of a particular asset well, such as a business interest. Some people would never want to see certain assets subject to the control of a former spouse. This is a very common estate planning goal in blended families. People often shudder to think that their property could come into the hands or under the control of a former spouse, and they are relieved when they learn about the methods to keep that from happening.

If you have a good relationship with a former spouse or partner, you can always name the person in your estate plan if you choose to give him or her something. It's completely up to you.

---

[31] You can read more about trusts related to this concern in Chapter 9.

Your Estate Planning Concerns

After you have evaluated and chosen your estate planning goals, it is time to consider possible risks and concerns in estate planning. In blended families, these concerns can be daunting. Below are some common concerns I've seen:

1. Choosing between a partner and the children

Often, choosing between a partner and the children is the greatest concern in estate planning for blended families. Who should receive what and at what time? Trying to balance the interests of the children getting an inheritance and a partner being supported after your death usually is a matter of the size of your estate. If your estate is large, it may be possible to do both. However, if your estate is modest, you may well have to choose. My best advice: once you have decided how you want your estate plan to look, take time to explain your actions to all parties so that no one is surprised after your death.

2. Planning for the payment and apportionment of estate taxes

If your estate is taxable,[32] how will the taxes be paid, and from which beneficiary's share will they be paid? Today, very few estates must worry about paying the federal estate tax. However, for those who do have to pay, the federal estate tax presents a huge concern due to the amount of the tax and the speed at which it is due.

Some people whose estates will owe estate tax choose not to worry about it and leave the problem to their loved ones. After all, they reason that they'll be dead and gone anyway. However, failure to minimize the estate tax could cause the sale of a family farm or business that took years to build. These people are much more likely to make estate tax reduction and funding a high priority.

In blended families, having the estate tax paid out of the share of another heir will negatively impact one side over the other, which increases the likelihood of litigation. This is something that you should discuss with your estate planning advisor first because most just assume that everyone wants to reduce

---

[32] Due to changes in tax laws, your estate may not be taxable today, but it may be in the future.

estate tax to the lowest possible amount no matter the side effects, which isn't always true.

3. Dealing with problem children

Should you leave assets to a child who has a problem handling money, or a problem partner, or a drug or alcohol problem? This usually means that a trust (which seems to imply "don't trust") will be helpful for that child. Problematic behaviors do not define a child as a problem. Address the behavior, not the person.

4. Protecting young or disabled children

How can you make sure that a new baby's inheritance is not totally used up by their cost of higher education, which older beneficiaries are already enjoying? Also, how can you provide funds to support a disabled child without the child losing federal, state, or provincial disability benefits? These raise distinct and separate concerns. Perhaps a healthy youngster needs to be educated, but a disabled child may need support and property management for the rest of his or her lifetime.

5. Caring for elderly parents

What if your parents outlive their own retirement savings? Suppose one or both of your parents survive you. Should you take care of their financial needs in your estate plan? Can you afford to take care of their financial needs? Elderly parents can present a serious impact both on your lifestyle and your estate planning.

Prioritize and Communicate

Once you have identified your estate planning goals and concerns, it is time to prioritize them. Using the Identifying Your Goals and Concerns checklist below, rank your goals from those you are most interested in to the ones that you are least interested in. Communicating these goals and concerns to your estate planner is essential because otherwise, your estate plan might not achieve what you want. Estate planning can be very complicated, but it doesn't have to be. The outcome of your estate plan will be improved if you properly consider your goals and concerns and communicate them to your estate planner.

Action Steps

Now that you've read through a number of possible goals and concerns for your estate plan, it's time to take action and determine your priorities and what matters to you. Complete the checklist below while referring to this chapter and see which sections speak to you and really touch on what you care about the most.

This is a great exercise to do separately and share with your partner afterward. You will learn more about each other and your concerns as they relate to the estate plan. Once you have a clear picture of what you each want to accomplish, you can read the rest of the book with a sense of purpose around how to best achieve your goals.

Checklist: Identifying Your Goals and Concerns

You can use this form to rate your goals and concerns. Rate these goals on a scale of 1 to 5, with 1 meaning "most important" and 5 meaning "not important." Give this form to your estate planners so that they know what is most important to you.

Potential Estate Planning Goals
_____ Retaining control
_____ Providing support
_____ Protecting assets
_____ Flexibility
_____ Retaining access to capital
_____ Transferring future appreciation
_____ Transferring of opportunity
_____ Skipping a generation
_____ Deferring estate and income taxes
_____ Qualifying for tax benefits
_____ Using gift tax exemptions and exclusions

_____ Maximizing usage of estate tax exclusions
_____ Facilitating charitable desires
_____ Tax predictability or finality
_____ Providing tax-deferred diversification
_____ Providing guidance and management
_____ Encouraging or discouraging behavior
_____ Leveling the playing field between those in control and those not in control
_____ Providing a mechanism for resolution of disputes
_____ Other (identify a goal not listed here): _____

Potential Concerns and Risks
_____ Choosing between your partner and the children
_____ Estate taxes
_____ Problem children
_____ Disabled children
_____ Elderly parents
_____ Risk of loss of control
_____ Risk of loss of access to capital
_____ Risk of doing nothing
_____ Risk of loss of flexibility
_____ Other (identify a concern not listed here): _____

Property Ownership: Means and Issues

This chapter introduces the variety of ways that people own property, either separately or together, as well as the various agreements that blended couples may enter with respect to their property.

Marriage Contracts and Property Agreements

Partners in blended families often enter marriage contracts (also called prenuptial agreements) prior to getting married, although these can be entered into after the wedding too (postnuptial agreements) if applicable state or provincial law permits. Additionally, unmarried partners often enter into property agreements that have many of the same provisions as marriage contracts. These agreements are usually signed and in place prior to a legal marriage. They are initiated for a variety of reasons and determine who owns what going into the partnership. At times, these agreements are required based on prior estate planning on the part of one of the partner's parents or grandparents.

Marriage contracts and property agreements often deal with the following issues:

- Classification of property owned coming into the partnership (e.g., community, jointly owned, or separate)

- Division of property on divorce or separation
- Whether property acquired during the marriage or relationship is to be considered community property, jointly owned property, or separate property
- Designation, ownership, and/or use of the residences the partners own
- Responsibility for separate debts
- Distribution of property on death, including placing restrictions on changing the estate plan after death of one of the partners
- Alimony or support in the event of divorce or separation
- Financial responsibilities in the partnership and the division of household financial responsibilities
- Applicable state or provincial law for interpretation or enforcement of the marriage contract or property agreement
- Whether alternate dispute resolution measures such as mediation or arbitration are to be used
- Whether the marriage contract or property agreement will terminate after a specified number of years of marriage or relationship
- Waiver of the spousal election (if married)

It is imperative that your estate planner review your marriage contract or property agreement, as it may limit your estate planning flexibility. You also may need to give your estate planner copies of all agreements that you have with former partners, as these agreements also may impact your estate planning. Many partners owe obligations to former partners, such as alimony, child support, or maintaining life or health insurance. These obligations can also impose restrictions on your estate planning, such as restricting testamentary freedom requiring legacies to certain persons such as children of a prior union. It is very important that your estate plan be coordinated and consistent with your marriage contract and property agreement.

Agreement issues

If you and your partner have a prenuptial or property agreement, chances are there were some emotionally charged conversations that occurred prior to the documents being signed. In most cases, the less wealthy partner didn't want to sign a prenuptial agreement or a property agreement because perhaps it reflected a lack of commitment, love, and trust from the wealthier partner. In reality, the estate planning professionals are the ones who typically encourage these agreements, because they are practical, safe, and sound business practices.

It is the duty of an estate planner, as an advisor, to do what they can to protect their clients from loss of property or other assets by anticipating possible breakdowns in the future. Given that the likelihood of splitting is greater in blended families than remaining together for life,[33] i.e., advisors are supposed to plan for that possible outcome as best they can. One thing I try to get partners considering these agreements to see is that if the roles were reversed, the other partner would be advised to do the same thing.

Without thoughtful communication and respect for each other's concerns while signing these documents, underlying hurt and resentment may arise. This will be even more likely if there are no stipulations for financially honoring the relationship over time, as this pain can lead to litigation. Often, we see that these agreements are frequently challenged after a couple splits. The typical allegations are that the wealthier partner misrepresented his or her wealth, or that one of the partners unduly influenced the other partner to sign the agreement.

The closer to the wedding date that a prenuptial agreement is signed, the greater the likelihood of a successful challenge to the agreement. The same is true if the partners are represented by the same lawyer. A careful estate planner should evaluate the likelihood of challenge to a prenuptial agreement. The estate planner will ask about any circumstances that are influencing the signing of this document at the time of execution of the agreement, which is important when considering the higher probability of divorce in blended-family marriages.[34]

Postnuptial agreements

A postnuptial agreement is an agreement that married partners enter into after they are married. The agreement contains the same provisions as prenuptial and property agreements. However, postnuptial agreements often deal with qualified retirement plan benefits. This is because a prospective spouse can't

---

[33] Mark Banschick M.D., "The High Failure Rate of Second and Third Marriages," https://www.psychologytoday.com/us/blog/the-intelligent-divorce/201202/the-high-failure-rate-second-and-third-marriages

[34] According to the 2010 US Census.

waive his or her interests in a qualified retirement plan (i.e., pension plan or 401(k) plan) until after he or she is married.

Spousal waiver of right to be the life beneficiary in a qualified retirement plan would permit the plan participant to make any person, such as his or her children, the beneficiary of the plan benefits. This rule is not applicable to Individual Retirement Accounts (IRAs), so it is common for a prospective spouse in a blended family to roll a qualified retirement plan into an IRA first to allow more freedom with the benefits.

Co-ownership Issues

It is not unusual for partners to co-own property prior to marriage. This property often includes real estate and other investments such as stocks. This property might have been acquired during marriage or began before the marriage and brought in to the union.

Jointly owned property can be owned either as tenants in common or as joint tenants with rights of survivorship. Jointly owned property is frequently acquired as joint tenants with rights of survivorship. The estate planner must review account titles and real estate deeds to determine whether a survivorship condition is present.

In my opinion, couples in blended-family relationships should not own any property with rights of survivorship because the property will pass to the surviving partner (i.e., surviving joint tenant) on the death of the first partner (i.e., first joint tenant). This will bypass the children of the first joint tenant to die, which usually is against the true intentions of that parent.

If the property is retitled as tenants in common, the surviving partner will co-own the property along with the deceased partner's estate. If the surviving partner desires and can afford it, the partners can agree that the survivor between them has the option to purchase the deceased partner's interest in the property, or he or she could be given a right to lease the property on favorable terms. The partners could also agree that the survivor between them would get to use the property for free for a period of time, such as two years.

Community Property

At the time of writing, nine states in the United States have community property laws. These states are Arizona, California, Idaho, Louisiana, Nevada,

New Mexico, Texas, Washington, and Wisconsin. Additionally, Alaska, South Dakota, and Tennessee have an opt-in community property regime, meaning that you can have a community property regime if you want one. Nevertheless, community property laws do differ from jurisdiction to jurisdiction. In other words, the community property laws in California differ from those in Arizona.

As a rule, unless they agree otherwise, property a married couple acquires during a marriage from earned wages is considered to be owned fifty-fifty as community property. It doesn't matter under whose name the property is acquired. However, property brought into a marriage, as well as property gifted or bequeathed to a spouse, is separate property. Generally, each spouse can pass off his or her half of the community property at death. However, a few community property states, such as Texas and California, have introduced a survivorship feature into the community property mix, so it is important that your estate planner review your community property titles.

It is not unusual for blended-family couples to have community property regimes with respect to property acquired during their marriage and separate property that each inherited or brought into the marriage. People do move periodically to other states, whether it is into a community property jurisdiction, or out of one. It is imperative that you provide your relocation history to your estate planner so that he or she can check to see if there is community property in your estate.

Community property has benefits for United States income and estate tax purposes that co-owned separate property in noncommunity property states do not have: unlike separate property, the surviving spouse's undivided one-half interest of the community property gets a new basis to the then fair-market value for the ***entirety*** of the property at the death of the spouse who is first to die. Contrast this with co-owned separate property in a noncommunity property state, where only the deceased spouse's interest gets the new basis. Consider the following example:

Bill and Mary are married and live in a community property state, and Bob and Alice are married and live in a noncommunity property state. Each couple buys a home for $100,000 in 1978. In 2021, each home is worth $1,500,000. In 2021, Bill and Bob both die. Mary's new tax basis in the home is $1,500,000, while Alice's tax basis will be $800,000 (Her husband Bob's new basis on his undivided one-half interest of $750,000—one-half of the home's fair market value at Bob's death of $1,500,000—plus Alice's original 1978 acquisition basis of an undivided one-half interest of $50,000). If each widow decides to downsize in 2021 and sells her home for $1,500,000, Mary will have no capital gains tax to pay, but Alice may not be so lucky. She'll probably have to pay capital gains tax due to the gain on the sale of the home.

Separate Property and the Perils of Commingling Property

Property that is neither community property nor jointly owned property is considered separate property. The difference between separate and community property is that generally one spouse is not able to make substantial gifts of community property without the consent of the other spouse. In blended families, most couples come into the marriage with each person owning their own separate property. It is easy to spell out the separate nature of these properties in a prenuptial or postnuptial agreement. This can also bring clarity to your estate planning goals going forward.

For the sake of ease and freedom from decision making with each other's personal property, I recommend that married blended-family couples have either a marriage contract or property agreement. I further recommend that a marriage contract expressly state that both partners agree that each is totally free to do their own estate planning without any need for input or consent by the other partner. Of course, this does not preclude communicating with each other and giving each other feedback and input. It is a way to honor that each of you has your own property and that you have the ultimate say on how it will be distributed. If property is neither jointly owned nor community property, it is your separate property.

What follows is probably the most valuable advice in this book, so pay close attention: *keep your separate property separate*. Do not commingle your accounts or keep "informal" track of things.

If you do nothing else, at least keep your property separate and avoid commingling.

While I'm aware that the majority of you have already commingled property and will continue to do so, there is potential risk in this. For example, Jack has two sons from a prior marriage and Jill has two daughters from a prior relationship. Jack and Jill commingled all their separate property in the course of their marriage, and at the time of Jack's death, Jill's daughters were able to successfully win a classification of property battle and receive more than Jack had intended, and Jack's sons did not receive the lion's share of Jack's estate that he owned prior to marrying Jill.

If you and your partner have been together for a while and have commingled your property, see if you can agree on a division of the property between the two of you now and at least identify which property belongs to whom. If this subject is too sensitive, or if the two of you can't reach an agreement, start tracking property going forward and write down what you consider to be your separate property and your community or jointly owned property.

How do these disputes over the classification of property arise? There are usually two ways that this can evolve into a dispute. The first is during a separation from your partner. If this event should arise, at least you are both alive to give your sides of the story, each with supporting proof. The second way that a dispute arises is after the death of a partner. The surviving partner often has the authority to initially say what belonged to the deceased partner if the surviving partner has been named the executor or administrator of the deceased partner's estate.

However, if the surviving partner's stepchildren (i.e., the children of the deceased partner) or the deceased partner's creditors disagree with the surviving partner's determination, they can contest it in court. Because the surviving partner made the initial determination, the court may be skeptical, particularly where the determination favors the surviving partner. That's why it is imperative that you maintain contemporaneous financial records. Financial records are usually difficult if not impossible to reconstruct after the fact.

Keeping accurate and correct financial records requires some discipline, but I find that the online record-keeping tools offered by many financial institutions and by bookkeeping programs such as Quicken and QuickBooks make this task simpler. Don't pay expenses from one account that should be paid from a different account. Take the time to properly classify income and expense sources or pay someone else to do it. The most important thing is that this gets done regularly. Put a note in your calendar for the first of each month to track and reconcile your finances to mitigate painful disputes in the future.

Another big mistake that many people make is relying on a marriage contract or property agreement alone to dictate property ownership. Just because you have a separate property agreement doesn't mean that your property is separate—it is up to you to keep it separate. If you commingle your property with your partner, it muddies the water as to who owns what and could indicate that you weren't both living by the agreement. You can't expect a court to uphold an agreement that the parties themselves didn't follow.

Contracts to Make a Will and Joint Will

Contracts to make a will are contracts whereby one party or the other, or both, agree to make a party's separate will in a certain way. A joint will is a will made by two people that generally can't be changed by the survivor.

Will contracts, both separate and joint, are governed by state law. Some jurisdictions don't permit will contracts or restrict their use to married partners, so you will need to check with your estate planning attorney to see the law in your jurisdiction. These agreements may provide for certain provisions to be contained in any will that a partner executes. It also sometimes restricts a partner's right to subsequently revoke or amend the will. Sometimes these types of provisions are included in a marriage contract or property agreement.

I see more desires to sign contracts to make a will or joint wills in blended families because the situations are generally more complicated than in single union situations. I'm not a particularly big fan of these arrangements because they unduly restrict surviving partners from addressing changes in circumstances that arise after the death of a partner. However, they can be helpful in situations in which a partner will only agree to give his entire estate to the other partner if she agrees to give it to his children after her death (and vice versa).

There are other ways to protect the testamentary intent of the first partner to die—namely, a lifetime trust for the benefit of the other partner as income beneficiary, with the children of the first partner to die being the principal beneficiaries. Using a life estate instead of a trust subjects the property to creditor's claims after the first partner dies, which you wouldn't want to see happen. A lifetime trust would keep this from happening and also remove the need for a will contract.

Prior Relationship Obligations and Benefits

It is not unusual for one or both partners in a blended-family situation to bring either obligations or benefits from a past relationship into a new union. These might stem from divorce judgments, or they can originate from separate agreements or contracts with former partners. It is imperative that your estate planning lawyer review all these documents.

As you plan together for the future, you must share your obligations from the past with your partner and estate planning advisors. These arrangements may restrict your partner's estate planning. For example, a divorce judgment may require a partner to maintain life insurance for the benefit of a former partner or children from a prior union. These are important details for your current partner to be aware of as you examine your present circumstances with your current obligations and make goals for the future.

If you have kept these from your partner out of fear of repercussion, know that sharing with him or her now, in a cooperative and humble way, will do much to strengthen your relationship going forward. You may have some upset to contend with around lack of trust in not telling your partner sooner, and this may cause your partner to wonder about what else you might be keeping from him or her. This is an opportunity to come clean, to treat your partner with respect, and to show him or her that, as you plan for your deaths, you're ready to take an important step toward greater trust and intimacy in your life together.

Types of Property

Introduction

Estate planning advice is often driven by the value and makeup of your property. Some estate planning techniques, such as the Qualified Personal Residence Trust (QPRT) in the United States, are limited to use with certain types of property (e.g., homes). Other estate planning techniques work better with specific types of property. For example, the Grantor Retained Annuity Trust (GRAT) usually works very well with marketable securities.

Analysis of property and debts is probably more important in estate planning for blended families than in estate planning for traditional families. In the typical blended-family relationship, the partners tend to bring separate property and debts into the partnership. This can differ quite a bit if the partners are not legally married as well.

Property can be owned in several different ways. It is imperative that you have it titled correctly and in accordance with your estate plan wishes. As a rule, it is not necessarily wise for blended-family couples to have pay-on-death accounts (discussed later in this chapter) or to own property as joint tenants with rights of survivorship (discussed in Chapter 3).

Nevertheless, this is what a lot of blended-family couples face because they didn't pay close enough attention when they were opening an account or buying a property. Don't make that mistake. If you have already made that mistake, you should correct the title immediately. This is one of the benefits of estate planning: catching and correcting mistakes before it is too late to do so. Having your property ownership in alignment with your estate plan is vital, as ownership supersedes what is stated in your will. Don't miss this important step!

Family Home

Your home may mean much more than a house to you and the members of your blended family. I address the family home as a specific asset because for many people, it represents the most significant property that someone owns. I've also run into many situations where the family home is a huge emotional issue for children of a prior union, especially if they were raised in the home.

There is also the issue of whether the owning partner wants his or her partner to continue to live in the home after his or her death. Finally, if the home is an emotional asset for the children of one of the partners, that can also make estate planning for the family home more challenging.

Since the home is such an emotional place, there is usually a lot of tension in estate planning around the family home. For example, there could be tension between wanting your partner to live in the home after your death and wanting your partner to live there with someone else after you are gone. There could also be tension concerning your children's right to inherit the home.

The family home should be treated as an asset just like any other piece of property, but it is one with some real emotional ties, especially if your children from a prior union are being raised there or were raised there. It is highly unlikely that if you die before your former spouse or partner, your children with your former spouse will continue to live there. They will probably relocate to live solely with your former spouse and even separate from their half-siblings and stepsiblings, along with other emotional changes such as switching schools or moving to a new city.

Home ownership for a blended couple in is one of the biggest issues in blended-family estate planning. There are at least four possibilities:

1. The home may be owned by one of the partners alone.
2. The couple may jointly own the home.

3. The home may be co-owned by one of the partners and that partner's children.
4. In some instances, the house may be co-owned by one of the partners and his or her former spouse.

It is not unusual in single-marriage estate planning for the partners to leave their interests in the home to each other so that the surviving partner will solely own the home. However, this is often not what a partner wants in blended-family estate planning, although the other partner may well exert pressure on the owning partner to leave the home to them for security and peace of mind.

There may be a situation of one partner lacking the physical or financial ability to maintain ownership and upkeep of the property after his or her partner's death. In this situation, it is important for the financially challenged partner to realize this and to plan for alternative living arrangements after his or her partner's death.

There are several ways to deal with the issue of the family home other than for the surviving partner to simply plan to move out after a partner's death. For example, the partners could agree that the surviving partner could stay in the home rent-free for a specified period of time after the partner's death in order to allow for an orderly transition.

Living Arrangements and Support

I've seen living arrangements in blended families that run the gamut, from one partner essentially paying for everything, to the partners judiciously keeping track of house and living expenses between themselves. I have seen division of expenses go so far as phone bills being divided with long-distance calls charged to the calling partner. A prenuptial, postnuptial, or property agreement also frequently provides instructions for living expenses.

It is not unusual for a couple to be living off the income of one partner. This is a situation that calls for some serious discussion about how the wealthier partner wants his or her partner to live if he or she dies first. How will this income be replaced if the earning partner dies first? How much salary should be replaced? For the living partner, how will the lifestyle change? Your partner will likely want to retain the same standard of living.

This becomes particularly challenging (and potentially contentious) if the surviving partner's desire to continue to live his or her current lifestyle means that the predeceasing partner's children get less. One of them may have receive less than you would like. This subject requires honest and direct communication between the two of you. There are also tools, such as life insurance and annuities, that can be used to address both of those desires.

Don't get bogged down if an issue has you stuck. Speak with a professional who can help you explore all your options and come up with a strategy where all concerns are addressed fairly.

Family Business Issues

Family business issues can confound and complicate any estate planning. However, in blended families, these issues magnify exponentially, especially if the couple is living off the family business. Suppose one partner owns a closely held business. If the owning partner dies first, the other partner may need to continue to live off the company after the owning partner dies.

Accordingly, special estate planning that may involve contracts such as buy-sell agreements, salary continuation, employment contracts, or other types of agreements will need to be done in order to protect the partner who does not own a share of the business, if that is what you want to do. Issues become even more complicated if you own most and your partner owns some, if you have children from a prior marriage in the business, and if your partner's offspring with you are also interested in working in and owning part of the business.

If, for instance, you own most of the business, and any of your children either work in the business or may work in the business in the future, this will impact who you will likely give or sell the business to or put in the role of trustee should you choose to put the business in a trust (which is one estate tax avoidance strategy). You may also want to consider how the different options you could choose might impact the job security and ongoing income of your loved ones at the time of your passing.

Lawyers tend to approach estate planning from the position of how to protect assets and how to protect people. You may want to consider the use of employment agreements, if for no other reason than to keep your children working for the business. Usually, if relations between the children and the surviving partner (i.e., their stepparent) are strained, the parties don't realize that they may need each other.

If, for instance, the stepmother is put in charge of the business, but she was not involved in the business during her partner's lifetime, she will need the children who have experience working in the business for guidance. Likewise, the children who work in the business need their stepmother, who is now their boss, whether they like it or not. If this is the governance that is chosen, it would be wise to make sure everyone is aware and on board ahead of time so that any potential grievances and resentments can be aired and cleared prior to the emotional impact of the owner's death. Employment agreements can take care of major family business concerns.

I've seen blended-family businesses of every kind, from those that remained successful to those that experienced financial ruin after the death of an owning partner. The latter seems to happen more often when no comprehensive estate and business succession planning was done. As the boss, you will need to evaluate your potential successors seriously and independently.

Quite frequently, either children aren't yet ready to run the business (if their parent should die in the immediate future) or the children don't have the temperament for management. However, your partner also may not be competent as a boss either, especially if he or she has never been involved in the business or has no business experience.

People don't often realize that if their business interests are left in trust and they make their partner the trustee, they've essentially put the partner in charge of the business. This could cause the business to flounder, especially if there is animosity between the surviving partner and the children of the deceased partner who work in the business. If half-siblings are involved, there can be favoritism to contend with as well. If stepsiblings and in-laws also work in the company, you've got an exponentially more complicated situation to contend with.

When people discover their roles in the estate plan at the time the will is read, there is the double impact of being ill-prepared to fulfill that role and the loss of the person they would have wanted to mentor them and show them what was expected of them.

For those of you in this situation, we encourage you to take time now to think these things through and discuss them with all relevant parties for their input and concerns. Describe your decisions when there's a chance to express your rationale. This will go a long way toward bringing more unity and harmony into your blended family's experience when the estate is transitioned.

Below are other particular family business issues you may have to face:

To sell or not to sell?

As the sole owner of a family business, you may be wondering how to protect both your partner and your children who are working in the business. Consider that you have an even tougher situation to ponder: Should you sell the company during your lifetime?

Many businesses are best sold during the owner's lifetime because the business is more valuable with the owner still around to assist the new owners if need be. Other owners choose not to sell while they are alive, hoping that their legacy will live on and that the business continue to sustain and support the family. Another reason they may choose not to sell is because their identity is so intertwined with being the originator, owner, and leader of the business that they cannot imagine what they would do without that role.

As an advisor who has seen what happens so often after the death of an original owner, I believe it is important for you to make an objective determination about selling. Value the company with you at the helm and without you at the helm. Get the data. This is a very tough decision, especially if you have children working in the business who may be expecting to take over after you are gone and who may not be welcome to keep working for the business after a sale. You would be wise to include them every step of the way so that they understand your thought process, and so they know you are aware of their concerns.

If you have decided to keep the business, or for some reason can't sell the company, you must put together a business succession plan. This plan will provide for your partner and also take care of your children, especially those children who are working in or who are dependent on the business.

Buy-sell agreements

It is advisable for all closely held businesses to have a business succession plan. One key element of a business succession plan is a buy-sell agreement. A buy-sell agreement is a legal written contract between some or all of the owners of a closely held business that details what happens upon the occurrence of one or more events, called "triggering events." Death, divorce, bankruptcy, disability, attempting to sell an interest of the company, and competing with the company are common triggering events, but they are not the only ones that can trigger a buy-sell agreement.

What's your succession plan for your family business?

A key element of a good buy-sell agreement is that it must prohibit transfer of any interest in the company except as provided in the buy-sell agreement. The buy-sell agreement must clearly set forth the applicable triggering events and what happens upon the occurrence of a particular triggering event. It is customary for a buy-sell agreement to permit transfers to certain person, often referred to in buy-sell agreements as "permitted transferees," despite the buy-sell agreement. Permitted transferees typically include certain family members.

In blended families, it is rare for the uninvolved partner to have any interest or involvement in the business. However, even if they aren't parties to the buy-sell agreement, I strongly recommend that uninvolved partners, particularly married partners, should acknowledge the existence of the buy-sell agreement in writing and sign off on the buy-sell agreement to prevent challenges after the involved partner's death.[35]

Less than all the children working in the business

Possibly one of the most difficult estate planning assignments is dealing with a closely held business owned by one partner in a blended family, where less than all the owning partner's children work in the business. It's usually a mistake to leave a business to all the children (including both those working in the business and those who are not) because the children who work in the business often come to resent the children who don't.

This is because the two sets of children usually have different interests. The children who work in the business usually view the business as their own and want to have the same liberties and same compensation that the parent enjoyed.

---

[35] For more information about buy-sell agreements, see my first book in the *Planning Your Future* series, *Buy-Sell Agreements: The Last Will & Testament for Your Business* (Paul Hood Services 2021), which is available in hardback, soft cover, and electronic forms from all major booksellers and from my website, www.paulhoodservices.com.

However, the children who don't work in the business are now fellow owners and also want money and other goodies from the company.

I've seen contentious issues between involved and uninvolved siblings, half-siblings, stepsiblings, and their respective in-laws where those in the company wished to reinvest earning back into the company for continued growth, and those not in the business wanted to have more liquidity and distributions. Therefore, it usually makes more sense to leave the business to the children working in it and leave other assets or life insurance to the other children and your uninvolved partner.

If the couple owns the business together but they have separate children, these issues can be even more difficult. Perhaps the hardest situation is where only one partner has children who are working in the business. Suppose the parent partner dies first. If the parent partner wants to leave his or her share of the business to the children, how do you protect the interests of the surviving partner? Hopefully, the situation won't change drastically between the surviving partner and the employee children in that case. Quite often, buy-sell agreements can be devised to navigate these treacherous waters. Issues related to buy-sell agreements become even more important when the couple in a blended-family situation co-own a business.

Retirement Plans

The interests of a partner in a qualified retirement plan can be a very difficult issue to deal with in estate planning for the blended family in the United States. This is because the Employee Retirement Income Security Act (ERISA) requires the nonworking spouse to be the beneficiary of a qualified retirement plan. This is often contrary to the desires of the working spouse, but the only way that the working spouse can name his or her own children as the beneficiaries of plan benefits is if the nonworking spouse waives in writing any interest in the plan, which rarely happens. This waiver can't be made in a prenuptial agreement, as it has to be made after the wedding occurs.

Retirement plan interests are fraught with their own challenges, even in traditional families, since the benefits are taxed when they are distributed, which significantly reduces their value. If the partners are not married, there is no requirement that the nonparticipant partner be named a beneficiary, freeing the participant partner to name anyone as beneficiary.

Do you know who the beneficiary is in your retirement plan? Is your plan up to date?

Individual Retirement Account (IRA)

Individual Retirement Accounts (IRAs) also make up significant portions of many people's estates in the United States. While traditional IRAs have the same income tax issues as qualified retirement plans, IRAs have more flexibility with respect to estate planning than qualified retirement plan accounts. The married partner does not have a federal right to be the beneficiary of an IRA. This is important in blended-family situations because the IRA account holder can build a trust that benefits both the partner (whether married or unmarried) and the children of a prior union.

Tangible Personal Property

The property category that probably creates the most hard feelings in all types of families is tangible personal property. This category can create significant litigation even if the property is not worth much financially. This category of property includes things such as family pictures, memorabilia, furniture, jewelry, crystal, silverware, and china.

In blended families, tangible personal property is often not carefully addressed in estate planning. As a result, the surviving partner gets this property, even though the deceased partner may have understood that the surviving partner would give the family property to his or her children. There is no guarantee that this wish will be honored.

If there is any advice to give about this type of property, it is to consider giving it to those you want to have it during your lifetime. Waiting until your death often doesn't accomplish your goal without very careful planning. If you give it away during your lifetime, and its value is within the $15,000 US federal gift tax annual exclusion that you are allowed each year, you also help mitigate some estate taxation of those particular items.

Bank Accounts

Money can be held several different ways, including an option to have a "pay on death" feature, in which the bank account holder names someone to take over that account upon the death of the account holder.

I don't usually recommend pay-on-death accounts to couples in blended families because this often conflicts with their estate plans. Remember, the account title trumps your will. For example, if your will gives your bank accounts to your children, but the accounts are held in pay-on-death or joint tenancy with rights of survivorship, your will may be meaningless. (You probably didn't realize the importance of dealing with bank tellers, did you?)

Action Steps

If you own a business and do not have a buy-sell agreement in place, that needs to be your very first action item.

For business owners who have an uninvolved spouse, take five minutes right now and ask the uninvolved spouse to acknowledge the existence of a buy-sell agreement in writing. Sign off on it in order to prevent challenges after the involved partner's death.

Now's the time to take a good, honest look at your property by answering the following questions:

- What is it you own individually and as a couple?
- What would each of you like to see happen with that property at the time of your deaths? Give space for each other to be heard. Enjoy learning more about each other and what you both see for the other partner and for the children in your lives.
- What components of this chapter are most relevant to you that you'd like to address first?

Come up with a plan that includes not only what you plan to address next, but importantly when you plan to address the issues. See if you can plan something fun to do after each step as a little reward for all the great progress you're making. Each small step is getting you closer to your goal!

Estate Planning Documents

Introduction

While estate planning, you will be reviewing, editing, modifying, and signing a number of documents. Most of these are legally binding documents that will put into effect that which matters most to you at the time of your death. This chapter will give you a clear understanding of the different documents that your advisors will be working with you on completing, as well as key considerations related to those documents. My goal is to give you clarity about what your advisors mean when they speak about these different documents while also giving you an advantage when it comes to your future decision making.

Wills

Wills are sometimes called "testaments" or "last will and testament." Believe it or not, a long time ago, there was a difference between *wills* and *testaments*: you gave away real estate by will, personal property by testament, and tangible personal property by will. Hence, the phrase "last will and testament" was intended for documents that transferred *both* real and personal property at death. However, this distinction is gone, so the two terms are now virtually synonymous.

Most people know something about wills, yet most people don't have one of their own.[36] Whatever the reason, I hope that you understand that everyone should have a will because a will is a formal legal expression of your wishes as to who will receive and manage your property, when your property will be delivered to the recipients, and who will look after your minor children.

One of the best things about a will is that you can change it at any time before your death (or until you become mentally incapacitated to such an extent that you lose legal capacity). While there are many books about wills, I'll cover the basics before focusing on the issues most important to blended-family partners.

First and foremost, the state laws of the person (i.e., the testator) putting together a will generally govern the will. As a general rule, there are limitations on what married partners can do in your will. Just about every state gives a surviving spouse a right to elect to take a minimum share of your estate, irrespective of what your will provides, unless you have a prenuptial agreement. Subject to the same caveats in the preceding sentence, you can leave your property to whomever you want, in whatever amounts, and subject to limitations as you wish.

Whether or not a will is valid depends on the place in which it was executed. Valid wills executed in one jurisdiction are almost always valid if you move to another jurisdiction. So, if you didn't change your will before death, the will still governs. This is important given that people often move between jurisdictions whether they be from state-to-state or province-to-province.

You can leave property to a trust that is set up in your will. These are called testamentary trusts, and they don't come into existence until you die, even though the will exists. Testamentary trusts can contain any provision that you want, subject to the laws of your jurisdiction. Some types of clauses in wills or trusts (e.g., those that restrict a beneficiary from marrying outside of his or her faith) are found invalid, as some courts deem them to be contrary to public policy of the applicable jurisdiction. Your estate planning attorney will be able to advise you on these matters.

---

[36] I delineated some of the fears and reasons why this may be the case in Chapter 1.

Wills and Minor Children

In a will, it is important to designate who will be the guardian of minor children if something should happen to both parents at the same time. One area of great concern to blended-family partners is designating who will take care of their minor children from prior relationships if they want it to be someone other than the child's surviving birth parent. It is very difficult to change this, unless the other parent has a significant problem such as drinking, abuse, or drugs.

If the other parent has been largely absent from the minor's life, you can see if he or she would be willing to relinquish parental rights because this opens the possibility of adoption, or at least makes it easier for the stepparent to become the legal guardian should something happen to the minor's primary caregiving parent.

Barring having parental rights willingly relinquished, the best that most blended-family parents can do in this instance is to state their desires in their wills and see if the court will go along. This presents a possible significant life change for the minor child, who may have younger half-siblings or stepsiblings with whom he or she is being raised. These are all factors for the court to consider and are not automatic determinants.

There are many blended-family situations in which the partner who is not the parent is the best option for the child, particularly when that partner has been very involved in the child's life for an extended time and when the other surviving birth parent has not played an active, engaged role. In this instance, another option is to get a memorandum of understanding from the child's other birth parent stating that he or she understands and agrees with the choice of the stepparent as guardian should something happen to the child's birth parent and primary caregiver. This can be added to the will for additional consideration by the courts.

Be proactive and make sure who you want to care for your minor children is designated and communicated the best way you can.

Wills and Probate

Many people believe that probate is a bad thing, but probate simply means supervision by a court. In the majority of jurisdictions today (California being a notable exception), probate is a very streamlined, efficient process of gathering the decedent's assets, identifying the decedent's debts, and passing the remaining property to the heirs according to the will or the laws of intestacy.[37]

In blended families with animosity in their family dynamics, probate is often a good idea because it protects everyone involved. Otherwise, if someone partial to one side is in charge, the chances of costly and unnecessary litigation are increased. Probate allows for a neutral third party (i.e., the court) to preside over your will and make sure that your wishes are carried out appropriately.

Trusts

A trust is a means of property ownership and management whereby the "grantor" or "settlor" transfers property to someone to manage for the benefit of the beneficiary. Trusts can be established during lifetime or at death.

Trusts are divided into several basic sections. One section clearly describes the identity of the trust beneficiaries, what they are to receive, and when they are to receive it. A significantly large section of most trusts deals with the authority and powers of the trustee.

Revocable Living Trusts

A revocable living trust is a trust that you establish during your lifetime. You frequently see these types of trusts referred to simply as "living trusts." By its very name, it is revocable, meaning that you can change it or get rid of it at any time. While most people don't need the additional complexity of a revocable living trust, these trusts are much more common in jurisdictions such as California where probate laws are antiquated, costly, and burdensome. In the overwhelming bulk of jurisdictions, people use wills instead.

Revocable trusts can have their place in any estate plan, and I see them used with more frequency in blended families because of the additional formality and protection that a trust can provide.

A revocable living trust contains many, if not most, of the same provisions that are in a will. Revocable trusts are just as easy to change as a will. Just because you have a revocable trust doesn't mean that you don't need a will so

---

[37] I discuss probate in great detail in Chapter 1.

that you can put into the revocable trust the property that you failed to put into the trust while you were alive.

Revocable trusts are often chosen over wills based on a mistaken belief that revocable trusts avoid probate and save taxes and costs. Unfortunately, except for only a few states and provinces, it is less expensive to use a will than a revocable trust, which is why wills are so much more prevalent. You can ask your local attorney about which option is the wisest to use in your particular jurisdiction, and why you might want to use one over the other, or both.

Irrevocable Trusts

Unlike revocable living trusts, which can be changed, irrevocable trusts can't be changed. Nevertheless, a well-drafted irrevocable trust should contain some flexible provisions that permit amendment, either by the trustee or by someone named in the trust as a trust protector or special trustee, to address unforeseen changes in circumstances. An irrevocable trust is a very broad topic, as irrevocable trusts can be established for many different reasons, such as holding gifts of property for a specified period of time.

The most important matter in the institution of a trust is the selection of a trustee. Remember, documents don't do the work; people do. In blended families, the selection of a trustee is a very difficult decision if there is or could be tension between your partner and your children. I strongly advocate the use of an independent third-party trustee for irrevocable trusts for blended families, especially if the beneficiaries include your partner and your separate children.

Beneficiary Designations

Beneficiary designations are related to nonprobate assets. They are extremely important because a significant amount of a person's wealth is tied up in nonprobate assets such as life insurance, Individual Retirement Accounts (IRAs), and retirement plans. Your will won't govern the transfer of these assets because they are nonprobate assets. The beneficiary designation governs, even if you attempt to leave those nonprobate assets to a different person in your will. It won't count and won't matter what you want.

This makes beneficiary designations so critical. In blended-family estate planning, it is imperative that your estate planners review actual copies of all your beneficiary designations—operating from memory here is dangerous and ill-advised. It is not unusual for a review of beneficiary designations to uncover stale beneficiary designations, such as a designation of a predeceased parent or an ex-partner. You may also have had additional children who aren't named as beneficiaries.

It is very important to name contingent or backup beneficiaries in case something happens to the originally named beneficiary. Note that financial institutions have been known to not be able to locate beneficiary designations and to have made errors in the naming of a beneficiary, so check with your bank to see what is on file because that is what will count.

Depending on the terms of the plan, it may be possible to prevent beneficiaries from withdrawing the entire amount at one time, thereby protecting the beneficiary from improvident spending. Usually there is a selection of options in this regard, and your estate planners can assist you with sorting them and picking ones that are right for your situation.

Powers of Attorney for Property and Financial Purposes

A power of attorney is a legal document in which you appoint someone to act on your behalf for whatever reason. These are very common in real estate transactions. In a power of attorney, you (i.e., the principal) dictate what activities your appointee (i.e., the agent) can do on your behalf. Your agent only has the authority that you give him or her, and no more.

In estate planning, the powers that are typically given to an agent are broad. The purpose of most estate planning powers of attorney are to try to prevent the principal from having to be subjected to court supervision in a conservatorship or guardianship.

Your power of attorney can come into effect anytime you want it to—either immediately or at some point in the future, such as when you are no longer able or willing to act on your own. These latter powers of attorney are called *springing* powers of attorney.

Springing powers of attorney can be problematic if the event that springs the power of attorney isn't clearly described. I almost never recommend springing powers of attorney because it is frequently difficult to prove that the event springing the power into effect has occurred. Often, the approval of medical doctors can be difficult to obtain.

The overwhelming majority of powers of attorney are drafted to go into effect immediately at incapacity and to survive your incapacity and last until your death. This type of power of attorney is referred to as a continuing, enduring, or durable power of attorney. Durable powers of attorney are very important in estate planning because incapacity is a much bigger problem to deal with and likely to happen before death. Therefore, a carefully planned durable power of attorney is a must, even moreso in a blended family.

By carefully "planned," I mean that the "regular" (if there is such a thing) powers in a durable power of attorney may be inappropriate in the blended-family context. For example, many durable powers of attorney make broad changes in their estate plans by revoking or amending trusts, exercising powers of appointment, giving away precious family heirlooms (e.g., silverware, china, artwork, and photographs), or changing beneficiary designations.

Such powers given to an interested party could cause your estate plan to be radically changed to the point of not being recognizable (in other words, not what you wanted). It is appropriate to put limits on an agent's authority in a durable power of attorney, particularly in a blended-family context where there may be conflicting agendas for the estate after each of you passes away. Clearly, the power of attorney given to a partner should automatically be revoked on separation or divorce.

Local law governs the legal form required for powers of attorney. Many powers can be generally given. However, some powers must be expressly included in the document. These powers include:

- To donate or give property to others
- To settle a lawsuit or refer a matter to arbitration
- To sell, buy, mortgage, or lease
- To accept or renounce an estate or trust
- To contract a loan, acknowledge a debt, or become a guarantor of a loan
- To draw or endorse promissory notes and negotiate instruments
- To enter into contracts between the agent and the principal
- To deal with tax authority (i.e., Internal Revenue Service) and state or provincial and local taxing authorities
- To waive accounting by the agent (however, it's unwise to allow an agent to not be responsible for his or her actions)

The most important thing to consider when choosing your agent under a durable power of attorney is: How much do you trust that person? Once a person is your agent under your durable power of attorney, he or she has the capacity to purchase real estate, sign contracts, or enter into other legal commitments on your behalf and, in theory, without you knowing about it, although he or she is obligated to act in your best interests.

Powers of Attorney for Health Care and Living Wills

Sometimes health-care powers of attorney and living wills are combined in documents called "advanced-care directives" or "health-care proxies." I usually recommend that the two separate documents, which serve very different purposes, not be combined, especially if you want to select different people to handle each of the tasks.

To clarify, a living will (also known as an advanced-care directive, health-care directive, or a physician's directive) is a legal document a person uses to make known his or her wishes regarding life-prolonging medical treatments. A living will informs your health-care providers and your family about your desires for medical treatment if you are not able to speak for yourself. It is an essential document for an agent under your health-care power of attorney so that he or she knows what decisions you want made on your behalf relating to discontinuing extraordinary life support. In your living will, you can designate who you want to carry out your wishes, and that person's role can be separate from the person who is your agent under your health-care power of attorney.

The person you name as your agent under your health-care power of attorney makes all your health-related decisions. The rules for health-care powers of attorney are a matter of local law, so your estate planning attorney can guide you on these matters.

Of all the documents you are considering, the health-care power of attorney and the living will are by far the most imperative for unmarried blended-family partners, as it ensures that the two of you can be there to make each other's medical-related decisions (or be part of the process, if you choose to appoint your partner and another trusted friend or family member with a background in medicine and health care).

Without a health-care power of attorney, and without a legally acknowledged relationship, your partner may be kept in the dark about important aspects of your health care and will be unable to participate in key decisions that may have a direct impact on his or her life (e.g., the caregivers who may be coming into the home, the location where you will be cared for such as assisted living or nursing home, and measures taken toward keeping you alive).

In a health-care power of attorney, it is customary for the person who signs the documents (principal) to give the following powers to the person of your choice (your agent):

- Engagements and termination: The ability to select, contact, and discuss your health-care needs. It also grants the agent the right to pay and/or terminate employment or discharge insurance companies and other health organizations, physicians, dentists, nurses, sitters, and other professional or nonprofessional medical assistance; select or change hospitals, health-care facilities, hospices, selection of insurance companies, or other health organizations, institutions, home care, nursing home, custodial care, or other places for medical treatment for the principal; and make decisions as to the manner and nature of treatments and services to be performed by any physician, nurse, hospital, or other institution for the principal.
- Representation: The power to represent you before any federal, state or provincial, or local health-care bodies, including, without limitation, medical plans and veterans' plans on any matter that involves your health-care and living arrangements.
- Emergency care and general power to consent: To consent and arrange for emergency care and other medical treatment for you, including, without limitation, ambulance and other emergency medical transport.
- Medical records: To have complete access to all medical records in any form pertaining to your physical or mental condition, and to reproduce and discuss with anyone, as well as the power to execute those consents and releases as necessary to obtain medical information and to discuss them with anyone.
- Power to consent: To make and execute all consents, refusal of consents, or withdrawal of consent to any care, treatment, service, or procedure, including, but not limited to, cardiopulmonary resuscitation, and to execute all releases from liability for any health-care provider which acts on your behalf.

Health-care powers of attorney can be very specific in the types of care that the principal either wants or doesn't want, including the following:

- Artificial nutrition and hydration: This is where you state under what circumstances you would choose to have life-sustaining procedures withheld (e.g., length of time in a coma without responsiveness, length of time in hospice care without hope of recovery). This can be a very controversial part of a health-care power of attorney when it comes to following certain religious guidelines. This issue is also dealt with in a living will; therefore, some people opt to not combine their advanced-care directive with their living will, letting one person take on this particularly challenging aspect and someone else to take care of the rest. Other people choose to combine the two in the hopes of not creating any confusion.
- Religious restrictions: Some religions, such as Jehovah's Witnesses, forbid blood transfusions. Other religions may have other restrictions as well. It is important to describe any religious restrictions for whoever is asked to be your health-care power of attorney, as he or she may likely face legal pressures in some instances.
- General intentions about mental health treatment: This includes addiction care and psychotropic drugs. This is also where to specify desired length of treatment stay, as well as the frequency and total number of treatment options, if this is an area of concern and likelihood.
- Organ and tissue donation: Some people are clear that none of their organs should be donated, while others want to donate their entire bodies to science. You get to state to what degree you would or would not like your organs to be donated. If this is a pertinent concern, explore with your attorney how to delineate this in a separate document.

Federal and state governments also place restrictions with whom doctors and other health-care providers can share information, so it is prudent to execute a Health Insurance Portability and Accountability Act (HIPAA) release, which will release your medical information to persons other than your agent under your health-care power of attorney. This is particularly important for blended families and unmarried partners who aren't the agent under the health-care power of attorney.

Ethical Wills

Your ethical will is your way to convey what you care about most to your loved ones. It is the time-honored tool for enduring personal expression. It is nonbinding, but it can accompany your will and/or trusts as a permanent place for loved ones to hear your "voice."

The resource that sets the standard for ethical wills is Susan B. Turnbull's *The Wealth of Your Life*. In it she shows in five easy steps how to craft your ethical will:

Step 1: Identify those you wish to address. This could be anyone from your children, your stepchildren, grandchildren, descendants (both through blood and through love) yet unborn, siblings, nieces, nephews, parents, spouse or partner, friends, guardians of your children, trustees, and even your agent under your health-care power of attorney.

Step 2: Consider your intentions and draft your opening lines. Many people treat this like a letter and start with a simple salutation and a brief about statement. Start with the end in mind as you consider what you would like the readers of your ethical will to have, and to feel, as a result of seeing your words.

Step 3: Reflect on what to include in the body of the letter. Make notes for reference. People find this part easier by breaking it down into sections. Some sections Turnbull suggests include: your history; values; perspective; estate plan and financial plan from a personal context; and your feelings of love, hope, and concern for your loved ones.

Step 4: Integrate your thoughts into an outline.

Step 5: With your notes to guide you, compose your ethical will.

Taking the time to do this will not only bring you and your loved ones peace of mind, but it will also go a long way toward mitigating potential hurt feelings and allowing for greater understanding as to why you set up your estate plan the way you did. Clearly expressing the context around your plan may allow the content of the will and other documents to be more fully respected and honored.[38]

Letters of Instruction

A letter of instruction, while not one of your formal estate planning documents, can be one of the most valuable legacies you can leave to those who will administer your estate after you are dead or incapacitated. It will give your executors and trustees a road map to follow to make their jobs much easier, less costly, and less time consuming.

In the letter, you can give detailed instructions and data related to where items are located and what exactly you want done with them. As you write your instructions, make it easy for your trustee and executor to find what they will need to fulfill your wishes easily.

For example, you could identify in one document all your various banking and other financial accounts and retirement plans, along with the names and contact information of the bankers and advisors who handle these accounts and where the check books and related cards are located. Don't forget to include your passwords for all online accounts. Remember, this should be printed and put in a safe, secure place spelled out in your letter.

If you are a beneficiary of a trust or an heir to an estate, mention this in the letter, as well as the contact information for who has been assisting you with those matters. Take care that this information is held by your estate planning attorney and/or in a locked box and do not share it with anyone else.

Additionally, list the names and contact information for your estate planning professionals as well as those you would like to be personally notified of your death; you can even say who you would like to contact them.

You could also make an inventory of your most valuable personal property such as diamonds, heirlooms, antiques, and artwork. Note the location where expensive watches, jewels, and memorabilia are stored. You will want to label sets of keys to all locks and vehicles and designate where these and the safe codes can be found when necessary. If you have safety deposit boxes, foreign accounts, or property, it is advisable to list those as well.

---

[38] In addition to Susan Turnbull's book, I highly recommend a book by Eric L. Weiner, Ph.D., *Words from the Heart: A Practical Guide to Writing an Ethical Will.*

Some people choose to specify how they wish the rest of their possessions to be distributed when their surviving spouse passes. Blended families need to be particularly creative in this arena due to different levels of attachment. Some family members may have grown to enjoy and love childhood belongings that don't carry the same meaning for their stepsiblings and half-siblings.

One strategy that I've seen work well in blended families (where there is a degree of amiability among all family members) is to ask what they'd like. Couples who are open to learning about what truly matters to their children when it comes to possessions can allow their heirs to inform them as to how to proceed with divvying up their possessions when the time comes. Sometimes, that time happens prior to death, such as when both parent and stepparent, or when a surviving partner, is admitted into an assisted-living or nursing home facility, thereby downsizing first to a great extent and passing on those belongings before death. This makes it even more important to have this conversation early.

The key here is that when you ask all the children in your lives what matters to them and what it is they want, assure them that you will not be offended and will not see them as entitled or greedy (these are common fears that keep beneficiaries from speaking up about what truly matters to them).

Burial or Cremation Instructions

While many of us have some idea of what we would like to have at our funeral or memorial service, very few of us actually include our preferred burial instructions. In many families, this doesn't matter because those plans aren't as emotionally charged as they can be in blended families. However, in blended families, failure to provide burial instructions could lead to very bitter fights between your children and your partner about what type of service and burial you wanted. Therefore, it is advisable to describe your funeral plans in writing and to let everyone know in advance exactly what you want.

It is not unusual for some family members, who are already grief-stricken at your passing, to want control of your funeral, ostensibly under the guise of doing what they think you would have wanted. Unfortunately, this often conflicts with what other family members think you would have wanted. Memories can change over time, as can desires and wishes.

For example, a father may have had a conversation with his oldest son years ago where he expressed a desire to be cremated. Since that conversation, he remarried a second wife who does not believe in cremation. If his wishes are not in writing, and if specific arrangements have not been made, that son is likely to hold true to the initially, long ago stated wish. The son may want to demonstrate that he knew his father better and was closer to him than his second wife. That father could have averted a lot of unnecessary pain and conflict by simply writing down exactly how he wanted his body treated at the time of his death.

I have also witnessed arguments over where a person will be buried, what kind of memorial service to have, where it will be held, and who will make the funeral or memorial service arrangements. This is why I advise you to take the time to describe in writing exactly what you want, and even make these arrangements in advance. Advance funeral planning is a great idea because if you don't do it, you run the risk of a dispute between your surviving partner and your children.

I've seen knock-down-drag-out fights over burial and cremation. Burial issues often involve the place of burial. Children may want a deceased parent to be buried in their hometown of origin and next to a predeceased parent. This becomes more complex if the partners lived in a different city, state, or province than where the deceased partner and his or her prior partner lived. Purchasing your plots (or urns) and settling all the arrangements well in advance will keep the agendas of others from creating conflict during a time of deep loss and grief.

There can also be arguments over whether a casket will be open or not. Families can argue for days over these and other issues, which delays the memorial service and interment or inurnment. Funeral homes often are left in a precarious situation when there are warring sides over the style of bodily disposition (burial versus cremation), place, and style of memorial service, and even what the deceased will wear in the casket.

I strongly recommend avoiding these arguments by delineating everything that you want for your funeral and disposal. While I realize that is not an easy task for you to face, I've seen how painful it can be when it is left up to the loved ones to figure it out on their own. In instances where there is discord among stepchildren and their surviving stepparent, delineation can save a lot of squabbling after your death.

Do key members of your family know your specific wishes for what you want to happen with your body after you die?

Write Your Own Obituary

Surprisingly, more feelings are hurt in obituaries than perhaps any other area of estate planning for blended families. The culprit is often the person who writes the obituary. Some write it with malicious intent, while others may have inadvertently left out someone.

On the more malicious side, in situations where relations between the surviving partner and the deceased partner's children are strained (or even hostile), I've seen one side or the other left out or even criticized in obituaries. These slights create wounds that often never heal and can permanently end relationships. I suggest avoiding this problem by writing your own obituary in advance. That way, you can name the people you wish and say what you want about yourself. If anyone's slighted, you're the one to blame.

If you're taking the time to write your own obituary, you could also name the publications in which you would like it to appear to make that job easier for the loved one in charge of executing that little detail.

Delineate Invites to the Memorial Service or Funeral

There are few things sadder than family members missing a funeral or memorial service of a parent or a partner, as this is a one-time event. In a blended family, if there is animosity between your partner and your children, you may assume that one group or the other will be excluded from your funeral or memorial service. This is a slight that will linger forever and could likely make a rift between two groups permanent. This is very rarely what people want, since most hope that the two sides will come together at least for the funeral or memorial service. However, I have seen surviving partners and children excluded from funeral or memorial services many times.

If you believe that there is even a remote chance that hard feelings will happen at your funeral or memorial service, consider delineating who is to be invited beforehand. In this way, you can invite and bring together all your loved ones for your funeral or memorial service, even if some of them don't want others there, and vice versa.

Sometimes, people allow short-term anger or long-standing resentment to cause them to make choices that they later regret that can never be rectified. I've seen that these can have long-term traumatic ramifications. You can avoid or at least minimize problems by listing who is to be alerted of your death and encourage everyone to be invited to your funeral or memorial service.

I strongly recommend having a conversation with the various members of your blended family while you are alive and well about your wishes for your funeral or memorial service. During those conversations, give them the chance to express their reasons why it would be painful or difficult or unthinkable to have certain people there. You may be able to begin to heal some of the pain that is keeping your entire family from being together during your lifetime, as well as forge the path for them to be together at the time of your death. You will be amazed at what can happen when someone feels truly heard and understood—his or her stance can shift, and he or she can begin to see new possibilities.

Action Steps

First and foremost, breathe in and out! This chapter is filled with a lot of heavy information and many action steps toward taking care of all your concerns. One step at a time!

PART II
BLENDED-FAMILY CONSIDERATIONS

The Estate Planning Players

Introduction

Estate planning is like a play. The star of the show, who also must be the director, is you. There are different schools of thought regarding whether your partner should be your costar, as there are both advantages and disadvantages to both of you sharing everything regarding your planning together.

While there is great value in working together in your estate planning, be cautious of the downfalls of including your partner in your planning.

Signposts of Need for Separate Representation

The following signposts indicate the need for separate representation, and hopefully an estate planner will point these out to you:

- One of you is childless but the other has children.
- There is significant disparity in wealth or income between you and your partner.
- One of you is economically dependent on the other.
- One of you does all the talking or appears to exert strong influence over the other

- The relationship is newer.
- A high number of past relationships.

These are not easy points to consider, and I ask that you neither gloss over nor ignore them. The more uncomfortable they make you, the stronger the indication that you should do some serious looking at what is causing you to feel ill at ease. I also want to reiterate that there are ways to have separate representation while also staying in communication. I encourage both of you to recognize that this is not personal and simply sound legal advice, and that you can take care of the concerns you each have as you go forward.

The goal in having separate representation is so your plans are coordinated effectively. You can share with each other along the way and ask for each other's input. You can do your plans in tandem and cheer each other on as you both go forward. You get to set the mood and the tone to how you approach your planning—whether you do it individually or as a couple.

Estate planning is a play that involves many people other than you. It is important to understand that your estate planning decisions will impact the lives and relationships of several people long after your plans go into effect.

Characteristics of Blended-Family Partners

Partners in a blended-family couple can be very different from each other. They can be close or distant in age, with different levels of sophistication and education backgrounds. They can have different health issues and concerns. There may be significant differences in the wealth and earning capacity. Some partners may have children, or be interested in having children, while others may not. The number and ages of the children may be vastly different, as well as the needs of each partner's children. Some couples may have joint children. Partners may differ in their relationships with the children of the other partner. A partner may have at least one living parent, while the other partner may not. One partner may have financial obligations to a former partner, while the other partner does not. Some partners may have several prior unions.

While most blended-family couples are married to each other, an increasing number of couples are not married. Some may have significant legal obstacles that prevent them from marrying. Some partners may coexist or contend with former partners. Some blended-family couples have been together for a long time, while other unions may be new. In some blended-family couples, one partner may have significant financial or emotional control over the other partner, while other couples are more evenly balanced.

Estate Planners

The second set of players in the estate planning play is the estate planners. Estate planners are human and bring their own perspective (i.e., personal biases, personalities, and preferences) into the estate planning process. Some estate planners are biased in favor of certain estate planning techniques. Many estate planners make judgment calls on the so-called boilerplate of their estate planning documents without discussing options with the client, whether those documents are beneficiary designations or legal documents such as wills or trusts.

You will like some estate planners as people, while others you won't like. Estate planners will feel the same way about you. Some estate planners will remind you of someone in your past you may like or dislike, and vice versa. Some estate planners are better listeners than others. Some are better at explaining themselves, seemingly having an innate ability to speak in understandable layperson's terms.

Estate planners have no formal training in the "human side" of estate planning. In their formal education, they are taught the intricacies of their area of estate planning, with little or no training in critical areas such as how to interview clients and how to deal with clients' emotions during the estate planning process. They pick up the "bedside manner" of estate planning on the fly.

The majority of estate planners purposefully shy away from the human side of estate planning, opting instead to focus in limited areas such as document preparation, life insurance sales, investment analysis, or estate tax reduction, which may not be in their clients' best interest. There is a big difference between an estate planner and an estate tax specialist. That difference is knowledge and awareness of the human side of estate planning.

There are usually multiple estate planners working for you at any given time, such as an estate planning lawyer, a certified accountant, and a life insurance agent. There may also be others such as an investment advisor, trust officer, or a planned giving professional. These people need to keep in touch with each other so that each knows what the other is doing. This often gets difficult if you forget that you are the director. The advisors may vie for the director role of your estate planning play.

This can be dangerous if left unchecked because some of the players may be at odds with what another has proposed. It is up to you to make sure all the choices being considered and utilized fit together and that they are not at odds with each other. It is important to find estate planners who can work well together and actually do so. Give all your advisors the same information and the right to talk to each other and exchange information relevant to your estate planning. The success of your estate plan depends on this.

Perhaps more than any other estate planning professional, estate planning attorneys face some significant and tricky ethical issues when representing a couple in an estate planning engagement, particularly when a blended-family couple is involved. Any good attorney will require you to sign a document frequently referred to as an "engagement letter," which describes the terms of representation. It may include what the attorney will do for you and how much the attorney will charge you for services. Some jurisdictions require attorneys to have written engagement letters.

One of you may already be represented by an estate planner, and the other may not be. He or she may agree to be represented by the same estate planner. However, an estate planner may be biased in favor of the original client, even if he or she is not supposed to be.

Other estate planning disciplines have ethical rules too, and those rules may well impact those estate planners' abilities to represent you together. As I indicated at the beginning of this chapter, there are many instances where it would be wise, and it is very much expected, to hire separate representation. I realize that this effectively doubles the cost financially, and it can take a toll emotionally.

My experience with blended-family joint representation has led me to see that there are several potential areas of conflict in joint representation; namely, disparities in age, children, and wealth. Unfortunately, hiring separate representation has proven to be sound advice with the statistics showing the separation rate among partners in blended-family situations are even higher than the first marriage divorce rate. The truth is that separate representation keeps things cleaner.

Children

The next set of players in this estate planning play is your children. Like the couple, your children are their own people. You may like some of them, but not the others. Some you can trust when it comes to money; some you cannot. You may or may not agree with choices some of them have made, such as careers or partners.

Some children have finished their education, while others may be in the process. Some live with you, full time or part time, while others may live on their own. Some children are dependent on you for their livelihood, while others are self-supporting. Some may have problems with drugs, alcohol, or gambling. Some children may have disabilities that require special attention for the remainder of their lives. You may be the primary caregiver for such a child, or someone else might be.

Some children may have partners, while others may not. I always counsel clients that a partner of a child always plays a very influential role. In other words, blood is not always thicker than water, or, in this case, marriage.

You may see different needs for your children from your estate plan, even from child to child. Many parents slavishly maintain a "treat them all equally" posture. Children tend to expect this, which is a product of the "what about me" syndrome. Other parents evaluate each child based on their perceived needs, or even whether the parent likes or trusts that child.

Some people will want their children to at least be aware of their estate plans while they're alive, while others will keep their estate plans a secret. I don't recommend the latter, as surprises tend to create hard feelings between the surviving siblings, not to mention a greater sense of loss around not being able to talk with you about it. Your estate planning decisions can impact how your children interact with each other after your death, so think about that when you're figuring out what to do.

Children also vary greatly in their relationships with your partner. Some children, especially young children, may view the other partner as a parent figure. Some children will detest and resent the other partner. Other children, particularly grown children, may have little or no relationship with your partner. Your children's relationship (or lack thereof) with your partner will impact your selection of fiduciaries as well as estate planning techniques.

Stepchildren

Why should your stepchildren be players in your estate plan? Because they may have significant influence on your partner's decisions in the estate planning process; especially if you two are using the same estate planning team. Therefore, including your stepchildren in your planning have do remarkable benefits for your relationship going forward.

You may be among the stepparents who want to provide for stepchildren, perhaps because they are young and may even see you as a parent, or possibly because they are the only children you've known and have raised. Or, you may not even know your stepchildren. Another thing to consider is that your own children may not know, or may not get along with, your stepchildren.

All of this is important because it can influence your choice of estate planning techniques or even whether you want to do joint estate planning with your partner. You may find that one of your stepchildren would make a good trustee or executor, and perhaps even a better choice than one of your own children, although this can be problematic for the stepchild if not handled properly with your partner and your birth children.

Partners of Your Children

Your children's partners can have significant influence, and this influence may impact what estate planning techniques you consider. For example, if you are concerned about a child's partner having a bad or disruptive influence, you may want to set up a trust with a third-party trustee for that child. Another consideration is how solid your child's relationship with that partner. If your child is in a short-term or rocky relationship, a trust may be needed to protect that child from his or her partner's possible malcontent. You may want to use a trust if you find that you don't trust your child's choice of partner.

Your Parents and Possibly Your Stepparents

It is not unusual for a parent of a partner to have a role in your estate planning play. Many people have an elderly or infirm parent to care for, which must be factored into the estate plan in case the parent survives you. In some instances, stepparents can play a vital role in estate planning as well.

It is also not unusual for a parent to have a significant estate of his or her own that could be factored into your estate plan, if for no other reason than to ask the parent to fashion his or her estate plan to allow you to disclaim your share so that it goes to your children instead.[39]

Grandchildren and Step-Grandchildren

Your grandchildren and step-grandchildren might play a role in your estate planning play. You may want them to receive a significant amount of your estate, pay for their education, or play some role in the management of your estate, particularly if the grandchild's parent has made what you consider problematic choices or has predeceased you.

Caution is always advised when skipping a generation down to grandchildren as there could be generation-skipping transfer tax. The rules are complex. This should only be done with the guidance of competent counsel.

Other Players

Third parties can play significant roles in your estate planning. Perhaps you would like a good friend, a professional advisor, or a bank to consider serving in a fiduciary capacity such as executor, trustee, trust protector, or guardian for a child. You should communicate with third parties in advance to make sure they will accept the role and do it the way that you want done. It is important to make sure the individuals you are approaching thoroughly understand what would be required of them in the particular role you would like them to consider.

Having this conversation before they serve is imperative because they could easily spoil your plan if they step aside. That's why it is important to name backup fiduciaries. Some friends may make great trustees, guardians, trust

---

[39] Caution: This must be done according to the strict dictates of the Internal Revenue Code. Essentially, the Internal Revenue Code doesn't permit you to expressly disclaim in favor of your children without the disclaimer being considered a gift by you to your children. Disclaimers are more fully discussed in Chapter 9.

protectors, or executors, but could encounter difficulties in their own lives down the road that make it impossible for them to serve. They also may not survive you. This is a common problem with naming someone in your own age bracket (or even an older person such as a parent). Be sure to name contingent fiduciaries just in case!

You could also approach a potential third-party trustee such as a bank to see if the bank will take on your trust. Some banks have minimum size restrictions for trusts; they will not take on trusts below a certain size. Banks are often particular about what your trust document says, so it is prudent to review the draft document with the bank's trust department to make sure that the bank will accept the document as written before you sign it.

Just because you named the bank as trustee doesn't mean the bank is required to serve. If the bank doesn't like the terms of your trust, or if your trust will be small, it can decline to act. Banks are not necessarily opposed to taking on trusts with complicated scenarios (and perhaps even contentious parties) like those in blended families, as long as the trust instrument is clear and the trust is large enough to warrant the difficulties. However, the last thing that a bank trust department wants is a small headache. Individual third parties such as professional fiduciaries, certified accountants, and other advisors also could be considered for a fiduciary position.[40]

Action Steps

Now that you know the players involved in your estate planning play, it's time to sort them all out.

I strongly recommend you put an appointment in your calendar to adequately capture all these players and their roles. Set aside twenty minutes and set a timer. Then, see how much you can get accomplished during that time. If you need more time, set the timer for another ten minutes, or schedule another appointment in your calendar to finish this step. Once you are done, put your completed lists in a place where you can easily access them when working on your estate plan. Be sure to celebrate in some little way when these steps have been completed and put away.

---

[40] More on the selection of fiduciaries, which can make or break your estate plan, in Chapter 7.

Reasons Estate Plans Fail

Introduction

You may ask why I included a chapter about the reasons estate plans fail. I believe that this is one of the most important chapters in this book because the simple fact is many estate plans do in fact fail.[41] While unfortunate, failed estate plans provide golden opportunities to learn lessons from the mistakes made. Read the following reasons carefully—one of them can happen to your estate while navigating the even more treacherous waters of blended-family estate planning.

Failure to Complete and Implement the Estate Plan

Introduction

The best estate plan ever devised is worthless if it is not completed and implemented. This seems rather self-evident, yet in my experience, many people walk around with incomplete estate plans. In other words, these people have

---

[41] According to research reported by Roy Williams and Vic Preisser in their book *Preparing Heirs*, 70 percent of estate plans fail.

started the estate planning process but haven't put the estate plan into effect. Many others blithely say "tomorrow" and have done nothing at all but think about it. Too often, tomorrow comes earlier than anticipated. Don't be one of those people.

In my experience, estate planning is a matter of inertia: once you start, you need to keep going until it is finished. Unfortunately, I see an inordinately high number of blended-family estate plans go uncompleted. I suspect that this is because some tough choices have to be made that require forthright communication.

Actions for Success

Plan for success. Take out your calendar right now and, if you have not done so already, sit down with your partner and decide when you both want to have your estate plans completed. Six months from today? A year from today? Be realistic and ambitious. One recommendation is to choose a date that is the same number of weeks away as the number of chapters in this book: 13 + 3 = 16 weeks. (The "+3" buffer takes into account that some chapters will require a bit more time to gather the data, and other chapters will have more thought-provoking work to contend with.)

Note each week which chapter you will tackle and the date by which you will complete the action steps. You can still go forward with the next chapter as you keep putting attention on the actions from the previous chapter. If you get bogged down, reexamine your intended date of completion and see what it will take on both your parts to complete your plan by that time. Pushing the date ahead again and again is not an option, as you'll likely get caught in the "tomorrow" scenario.

Failure to Provide Complete and Accurate Information to Estate Planners

Introduction

It is axiomatic that you should provide complete and accurate information to your estate planners. However, the simple fact is that many people neglect, withhold, or refuse to turn over key pieces of information that, had the estate planner been apprised of that information, would have changed the advice or recommendations given.

Why would someone intentionally withhold important information? Perhaps you think that the information is too embarrassing or will give too much financial information that will alert the taxing authorities. Whatever the reason, it is the wrong approach because it has been my experience that all the information comes out anyway after you're dead. Just like you can't take your property with you when you die, you can rarely take what you know about your affairs to your grave, especially if it affects someone still living. I also see a higher-than-average number of blended-family estate plans fail due to withheld information, and I suspect that some of this is due to a number of different factors, including the following:

- There may not be enough trust and transparency between the two partners who've chosen to use only one estate planner.
- The complexities of the estate planning process bog down the couple so they choose what they believe is enough information as a way to try to streamline the process, instead of digging up all the information and data that is needed.
- There may be sufficient shame and guilt about past choices and decisions that have one or both partners unwilling or unable to openly share all the details with their advisors.
- The individuals may not know what to do about aspects of their estate, so they end up not talking about it because they don't know where to begin.

Actions for Success

- Take an honest look at the reasons above for why documents and needed information do not get provided. Could any of those reasons be true for you? Now's the time to be clear and determine if you will have the ability to work with one estate planning advisor together, or if you will need to work with separate ones.
- Locate and collect all your documents and data for your advisors.

- What one document would help support this process the best? Write it down and make a goal for when you will have that document in front of you.

Failure to Coordinate

Introduction

People often try to do piecemeal estate planning (e.g., a life insurance policy here, a will there) but no coordinated estate plan. Here's an example of a failure to properly plan in a coordinated way. Suppose your wills are drafted to pay estate tax at either's death, but your life insurance policy is a second-to-die life insurance policy, which doesn't pay its benefits until both insured parties die. Your will needs to be coordinated with all your other plans, whether it's your life insurance, lifetime trusts, or buy-sell agreements.

Actions for success

After you have chosen all your advisors and created your list with all their contact information, you can do the following:

- Give each advisor copies of the information along with permission to coordinate and speak with your other advisors.
- Convene a roundtable meeting with your advisors together where give an overview of the data and goals and create a plan together.
- Have regularly scheduled, brief conference calls with all of your advisors at one time, learning what has been completed, what the next action items are, and what is required of you.

Failure to Communicate about Your Estate Plan

Introduction

It may not be evident why communication of your estate planning intentions with your loved ones is so important, but our experience and research have shown us unquestionably that it is. The number one reason estate plans fail is a lack of communication and trust among family members as it relates to the family's wealth, assets, finances, and estate plan.[42]

Family members and perhaps others have expectations about an inheritance, whether they should. When these expectations are not met after your death, they may leap to some conclusions that may not be true, and they may take some actions that are unnecessary. Remember the story I told you about the parent who failed to communicate to a child the reason they had left that child out of their estate plan; the reason may have been legitimate and accepted by that child, but that unfortunate oversight left the child wondering for the rest of her life whether her parent loved her less and either suffering heartache or worse yet ending their relationships with her siblings over this slight.

Other possible unnecessary outcomes that could occur after your death include resenting some or all the receivers of power or property, as well as litigation in contesting or simply prolonging the matter. I firmly believe that good communication can prevent or at least minimize these types of actions by reducing animosity and creating buy-in with all family members so that everyone is clear about what to expect at the time of your death.

When I say communication, I mean exactly that. You don't have to ask your family for their input, although I have found that this is a good idea most of the time. Your estate plan is yours alone: it is not a democracy. However, communicating why you're doing what you are doing in your estate plan can prevent broken relationships after your death as well as costly litigation where no one wins but the lawyers. In blended families, because of the complexity and tenuousness of some relationships to begin with, communication is even more encouraged because, again, more blended-family estate plans seem to fail on this score. Communication can be made during your lifetime or shortly after your death. It can be in writing, recorded, or merely oral. The big thing is to just do it.

I have experienced pushback from clients when I enthusiastically encouraged communication. Some thought that it was simply none of their heirs' business. Others were scared at the prospect of confrontation. However, after relating some horror stories of the things that can happen if they don't communicate the reason for the estate planning decisions, the overwhelming majority

---

[42] From Roy Williams and Vic Preisser in their book *Preparing Heirs*.

did so, and most of them found the experience to be pleasant, giving them significant peace of mind.

Actions for Success

- Look at one aspect of your estate planning process with which you'd like to open a conversation with all the children in your blended family. Perhaps it will be about education or maybe about the family home.
- If you feel that communication is needed but you do not feel skilled enough to proceed on your own, consider hiring a coach to work with you to build skills and to facilitate one or multiple family meetings, depending on how large and complex your estate is.

Incomplete or Incorrect Beneficiary Designations

Introduction

As I've said several times in this book, and it can't be said enough, deficient or even missing beneficiary designations are the culprits for many failed estate plans. Too often, people don't give enough thought to the ramifications of their decisions about beneficiaries of life insurance, retirement plans, and Individual Retirement Accounts (IRAs), even though these constitute the majority of the wealth for most people. These documents are often hurriedly completed. The first step is to gather all the beneficiary designations that are on file with the company or plan provider. You can't work from memory here. I have heard some horror stories where companies lost the original beneficiary forms, which caused some serious and unfortunate chaos.

After you gather all your beneficiary designations, sit down with your estate planning attorney and coordinate your beneficiary designations with your overall estate plans. You should also have contingent beneficiary designations in case the original beneficiary dies before you do. You need to describe with specificity what is to happen if, for example, one of your beneficiaries dies but leaves children. Who gets that share? Is it the surviving beneficiaries (which is what most plans provide)? Or do the children of the predeceased beneficiary, who often are your grandchildren, get the share?

Consider the following example: Suppose that Bill has three sons, Moe, Larry, and Curly, and Moe dies before Bill. Moe has a son, Shemp. When Bill dies, it is discovered that he has not changed his beneficiary designation to reflect Moe's death. What happens to Moe's share? Is it simply divided between Moe's surviving brothers, Larry and Curly, or does Shemp step in and take Moe's share? Your beneficiary form should describe your intentions in this regard, or the terms of the retirement plan, which you probably don't know. The bottom line: describe what you want to have happen and don't leave it up to chance.

You must give this significant thought and seek competent professional advice with these matters. Unfortunately, blended-family estate plans are more deficient in this area than most, again because of the complexity and often torn agendas with "yours, mine, and ours" aspect to consider.

Actions for Success

- Pull together your beneficiary designations that are on file with the plan administrator or plan provider.
- Review all the designations and make sure that they are up to date and reflect what you want your estate plan to do. These must be in alignment.
- Make these designations fully available to your estate planning team and make sure key beneficiaries are aware of designations if being a beneficiary will have an impact on the beneficiary's estate planning as well.

Failure to Keep Estate Plan Current

Introduction

Even the best estate plans can go stale if not revisited regularly. Sometimes this is due to law changes. Usually, though, it is due to life changes. In blended families, I've seen many situations where a former partner received a large share of the deceased partner's estate (i.e., the decedent), life insurance, or retirement plans because the decedent failed to update the estate plan after the separation.

Some jurisdictions have laws that automatically remove a spouse as an heir at the time of divorce, but these laws may not apply to life insurance or retirement plans. Unmarried partners who separate are at a greater risk of having a former partner share in their estates without affirmative action on their part to change their estate plans on a split.

Actions for Success

If you have not done so already, now's the time to review the beneficiaries of all your various estate planning documents. You may be surprised by what you find. As you review and make any updates and changes, keep track of this information in an easy-to-locate place so that you have ease of access when the time comes to make changes. I recommend putting this information in your estate planning binder so that it is with everything else and easy to find.

Choosing the Wrong Trustee or Executor

Introduction

Many people ask what the difference is between an executor and a trustee. The ultimate difference is that the job of trustee almost always lasts much longer and requires more complexity than the job of executor.

The executor's role is intended to be temporary and only lasts while the estate is being administered. The executor's administrative tasks include, but are not limited to, the identification and gathering of the assets in the estate, payment of the decedent's debts, taxes, and distribution of the assets to the ultimate recipients—whether outright to individuals, trustees, or pursuant to the laws of intestacy. If the executor is guided by an attorney who possesses the requisite skill in estate administration, not much skill may be required of an executor. This couldn't be further from the truth for a trustee. Trustees must possess many more skills.

Ultimately, estate plans are administered by people. The best estate planning documents on Earth won't save an estate plan managed by the wrong people. How do you know who the right people are? The first thing to consider is whether someone is very competent in financial matters. The most well-intentioned, good-hearted soul who can't manage finances is an accident waiting to happen as a trustee or executor. Evidence of financial ability is a good indicator; one who can't manage his or her own finances is more likely to be tempted to access the money under his or her control that belongs to other people.

Executors and trustees are frequently referred to as fiduciaries. The prospective fiduciary must either be a great record keeper or be willing to farm that out to professionals. I also suggest that a prospective fiduciary be at least more than self-sufficient to prevent the temptation to poach the property of the estate or trust and to be able to cover any mistakes that he or she makes in the administration of the estate or trust. People frequently don't consider the need to have a bond for a fiduciary, but it often is a good idea to require one, especially for trustees unless you choose a corporate fiduciary such as a bank or trust company.[43]

You will need to consider a prospective fiduciary's age as well. Someone who would be a terrific choice but who is older than you is probably not who you want; chances are he or she won't survive you. If you're considering a corporate fiduciary, you probably want to investigate the experience in estates and trusts of the employees of the prospective fiduciary. One thing to be aware of as you make your considerations is the degree of turnover in the corporate environment, as you may choose a great employee who ends up leaving the company prior to your death.

One significant criticism of corporate fiduciaries is that they are poor communicators, bureaucratic, and fail to exercise the discretion given to them, especially when it comes to distributing property or income to a beneficiary. Frequently, the best option is to have a person and a corporate fiduciary as co-fiduciaries, with the corporate fiduciary taking care of the investments and taxes, and the individual fiduciary taking care of the needs of the beneficiaries, although this is truer in my experience for trustees rather than executors.

You need to consider whether the prospective fiduciary will have a conflict of interest that might cause him or her to favor himself or herself over the other beneficiaries. While this is not a totally determinative factor in traditional, nuclear families, it can be a real problem in a blended family. Stepchildren tend to be more demanding and more litigious when a surviving partner serves as a

---

[43] For more information about bonds for fiduciaries in the United States, see www.suretybonds.com/surety-bonds.html.

fiduciary for the stepchildren, usually because the stepchildren view a surviving stepparent as a rival and regard them with distrust.

You should also consider how well the prospective fiduciary communicates, as a very frequent source of conflict between fiduciaries and heirs is miscommunication, or incomplete, inadequate, infrequent, or otherwise poor communication.

How flexible is the prospective fiduciary? This is especially important if you're going to give the fiduciary significant flexibility, which usually is a good idea so that he or she can address unforeseen future changes.

Another quality that to look for in a fiduciary is if he or she is strong enough to withstand what can be very belligerent beneficiaries who want all their money now. If the trustee capitulates to the haranguing of beneficiaries (or their lawyers), the purpose of the trust can be compromised, which can be devastating.

It is usually a good idea to put a system of checks and balances on fiduciaries to level the playing field, particularly with a corporate fiduciary or where a beneficiary also is a fiduciary. This also is particularly true for blended-family situations. I usually recommend the following:

- Require accounting records to be provided no less than annually (local law often requires this).
- Allow the beneficiaries to replace a fiduciary with another fiduciary under specified circumstances.
- Require the consent of beneficiaries or others prior to the fiduciary taking certain significant actions (e.g., selling a family business).
- Impose a trust protector (who is almost always an individual and who is sometimes called a "special trustee" or "trust advisor") between the trustee and the beneficiaries for both flexibility as well as to rein in a wayward fiduciary or to remove a fiduciary.[44]

Finally, and this could be its own separate mistake—a failure to name successor fiduciaries or, at least, a means of appointing successors. This is particularly true in blended families where a beneficiary, be it your partner or

---

[44] Note: There are myriad significant tax reasons for naming an independent trustee depending on how you want to structure the trust. You will need to be assisted in this area by your estate planning attorney.

one of your children, also is serving as a fiduciary, and he or she either passes away or is no longer able to perform the duties. Consider who will take over the person's role and specify your choice.

Actions for Success

- If you have already selected your executors and trustees, congratulations—this is a major accomplishment in and of itself. Now, use this section to make sure that the people you have chosen are right for the position. Do they meet all the criteria? Is there a conflict of interest?
- If you have not selected your executors and trustees, now's the time to do so. You are empowered now to select the right person. Consider all your options and make your choice meets all the requirements given above to assure that your estate will be managed well and with minimal challenges.
- Once you've narrowed down your choices, consider who will be your first choice and who your alternatives are. Once you get firm commitments, you need to choose the successor fiduciaries and approach them to get their commitment as well.

Bad Estate Planning Advice

Introduction

Unfortunately, many estate plans also fail because people picked the wrong estate planners or the estate planners that they selected gave incorrect or bad advice. Sometimes this is malpractice, but quite often it is not.

Don't hesitate to bring in another member to your estate planning team or to change estate planners, although you should have good reasons for doing the latter—not liking their advice often isn't a good enough reason. Estate planning is not a job for the dabbler. You need and must have a team of people who do almost nothing but estate planning.

Too often, people want to use their divorce lawyer, or a lawyer who helped them in a lawsuit, or a family member who might be less expensive than hiring a professional. This is usually a bad idea. Using the same lawyer in a family situation might be a conflict of interest for the lawyer. In blended-family situations, it may be problematic for you to use your partner's estate planning attorney because of the possibility of divided loyalty for the attorney or favoring the longer relationship.

Actions for Success

In Chapter 11, I go into detail about how to select the right estate planning attorney for you, including resources, questions, and areas to consider. Study Chapter 11 and use it as a guide in finding the right advisors for you. Make sure your advisors understand the complexities of blended-family issues and that they have had experience in this area when it comes to estate planning.

Elections against a Will

Introduction

This section applies to married partners only. It is especially relevant for those spouses who cannot agree on how to divvy the estate in ways that feel fair to both. Depending on your jurisdiction, a spouse may be able to claim rights up to one-half of your estate unless that right has been properly waived in a valid prenuptial or postnuptial agreement.

You'll have to ask your estate planning attorney the ins and outs of this area (e.g., how much the spouse can get, how he or she can get it, and what is covered in your estate that is potentially exposed to a spousal election). It's also imperative that you get advice from an expert in nuptial agreements since these are often challenged at death if the spouse doesn't get what he or she thinks that he or she deserves.

Actions for Success

- Consult a local estate planning attorney who is well versed in the phenomena of elections against a will. Not only will you learn more about this aspect of estate planning, but you will also learn a lot about how that advisor works with clients by how he or she answers your questions. Does the person explain the answers in ways you understand? Does he or she understand why something like this might be

important to consider? Does the person listen to you, or does he or she steer you toward what he or she thinks is the better choice before getting all the relevant facts?
- Review your marriage contracts and property agreements with the same attorney and see if they cover your concerns adequately or if there is vulnerability. If you do not have either of these contracts or agreements, consult with the attorney about how you might get a postnuptial agreement at this stage or whether there are other documents he or she recommends instead.

Postdeath Will and Trust Challenges

Introduction

Few things delay the administration of an estate longer than postdeath challenges to the estate plan. As I've discussed previously, it has been my experience that a significant amount of postdeath challenges almost always arise from a failure to meet the suing person's inheritance expectations. However, there are people who, out of pure spite, will challenge an estate, will, or trust. I see far more of both categories in blended-family situations.

The majority of postdeath challenges fall into two basic categories:

1. Challenges based on a claim that the decedent was not in his or her right mind when he or she made his or her estate plan
2. A claim that someone unduly influenced the decedent to make the estate plan the way that it was made

It is the latter category that more blended-family estate planning partners must be concerned about due to the frequency of discord between stepparents and stepchildren. This is one reason partners in blended families choose to do their estate planning independently of each other and their children. While this choice may cause the "undue influence" claim to seem unfounded, it does not preclude a disgruntled heir from suing anyway. As I've shown already, effective communication is the key to mitigating litigation in the end.

Actions for Success

- If you see the value of open communication, and also see that your family needs additional support in having these conversations, it might be wise to hire a facilitator or coach who specializes in estate planning and family dynamics.
- If you believe there's no way your family will ever be in the same state together, let alone the same room, and that open communication is out of the question, speak with your advisor about possible clauses you can utilize in your estate plan to minimize the likelihood of litigation.

Too Much Joint-Tenancy Property

Introduction

Joint tenancy can be the prime enemy of estate plans because property that is titled as joint tenants automatically passes to the surviving joint tenant on the death of the first joint tenant. In situations where this may not be your intention, or if it conflicts with what your other estate planning documents provide, joint tenancy will override this, and your plans become irrelevant where those assets are concerned.

Action for Success

Now's the time to review your property and how it is owned, if you haven't done so already—and not just real estate, as it may refer to bank accounts as well. Take time to look at what you own and how it's owned and determine if you need to restructure some or all your joint tenancies. If you find that a property is titled as joint tenants and you wanted it to go to other heirs, you may need to either retitle it or reconfigure other aspects of your estate to take care of your original goal for how you wanted to treat your heirs.

Failure to Properly Plan for Disability

Introduction

Just because you have a living trust or a property power of attorney doesn't mean that you are adequately prepared for disability. It is important that your power of attorney document, especially if it is a springing power of attorney, clearly describes a procedure for "springing" the power of attorney into effect. The same is true for the activation of a successor trustee in a living trust. If your document doesn't activate a successor, you may have to go to court and incur that expense and time delay. Additionally, if you have a living trust, your property power of attorney and your living trust must be coordinated with each other.

Actions for Success

- First and foremost, make sure you have a power of attorney in place. If you don't, it is essential and should be noted on your calendar as a high priority.
- Review the powers of attorney section in Chapter 6 and determine if yours should be springing or not.
- Make sure that your power of attorneys is designed as you intend and that you have clearly and specifically delineated what, if any, will trigger springing into effect.
- For those of you with a living trust, or those who intend to create a living trust, make sure that your property power of attorney and your living trust are coordinated with each other.

Overfunding of the Federal Estate Tax Marital Deduction Portion

Introduction

If you are married and worrying about the United States federal estate tax, overfunding what effectively passes to the surviving spouse could cause you to underutilize your applicable exclusion amount. Of course, portability (which allows spouses to transfer unused estate tax applicable exclusion amount to the surviving spouse) may save the day, although the law of portability has several traps for the unwary. One of the biggest traps is what happens if the surviving spouse remarries; this law is somewhat complicated, so your estate planning attorney can explain it further if need be. It is strongly advisable for married partners in blended-family relationships to separately utilize their respective estate tax exemptions.

Action for Success

Make sure you understand fully how to best utilize your respective estate tax exemptions and work with your advisors to make sure they are implemented according to your wishes.

Relying on a Beneficiary to Do the "Right Thing"

Introduction

Believe it or not, a not insignificant number of people initially simply wish to leave it up to someone else to determine who gets what out of their estates. For example, some leave their estates to their partners or to one of their children with nonbinding instructions as to how they wish the estate to be divided. Most of the time, these people truly believe that the designated person will do the "right thing" and divide the estate either equally among their heirs. Or, they believe the designated person will know and do what the person wanted them to do with the property without explanation.

Sadly, this rarely happens, so the designated person often keeps the entire estate. This type of attitude can be particularly dangerous in blended families since there is less incentive for the designated person, be it a child from a prior relationship or a surviving partner, to share property with their stepfamily.

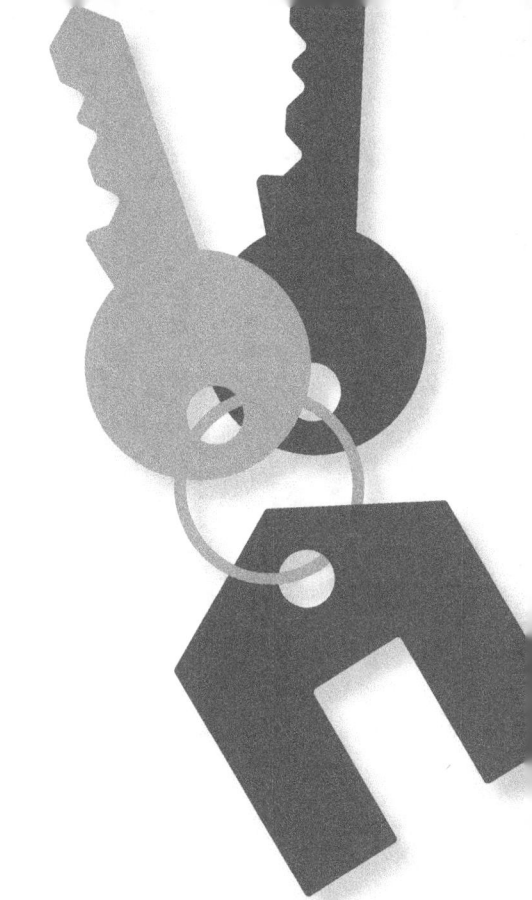

PART III
BLENDED-FAMILY ESTATE PLANNING TECHNIQUE ISSUES

Lifetime Estate Planning

Introduction

This chapter will discuss lifetime estate planning options, focusing on the application of those techniques in blended-family situations. Simply put, lifetime estate planning is related to mechanisms by which you can transfer some of your estate during your lifetime. These techniques are used to mitigate estate taxes for you to witness the benefits loved ones receive and the ability to respond when there is a need or request from one of your blended-family members in a way that supports you and your overall estate goals with regards to your estate.

This chapter will review the potential estate planning options that are available during one's lifetime. The descriptions are not intended to be an all-encompassing discussion of each particular technique. If you are uncertain about a particular technique, or if you have questions that the discussion doesn't answer, please consult a book on estate planning techniques.[45] My discussion of each technique is intended to focus on the use or advised nonuse of that estate planning technique given the nuances of blended families.

---

[45] Recommendations can be found in the Appendix.

For ease of accessing the information most relevant to you, the discussion is broken into wealth categories. These wealth categories are not set in stone and only represent my opinion. In other words, these categories don't necessarily mean that if you aren't in a particular wealth category, you can't use that particular estate planning technique. They just mean that, in my opinion, certain techniques work better in certain wealth categories—reasonable minds can and will differ on these categories.

It also doesn't mean that if you are in one of these wealth categories, you should use all these techniques. You may have personal circumstances that dictate that you do something else, or even nothing at all. I offer them as guidelines help you sort all your options. Your advisor will be able to assist you in determining what makes the most sense for you and your blended family.

Irrevocable Lifetime Estate Planning

Before discussing the various techniques related to lifetime estate planning, I want to emphasize one aspect that applies to everyone: *general admonition against irrevocable lifetime estate planning.*

By irrevocable lifetime estate planning, I mean estate planning that, once done, usually can't be undone without a lot of trouble and potential expense. Estate planners often break down lifetime estate planning considerations to whether the client can afford to make lifetime gifts. Estate planners often attempt to make the determination regarding what the client can afford to do with respect to lifetime gifting, instead of having the client make that determination themselves.

Sometimes, the estate planner's advice is couched in terms of what the client cannot afford *not* to do. This is particularly true with annual exclusion gifting (i.e., gifts of $15,000 per year in 2021 in the United States to an unlimited number of people) as well as the applicable exclusion amount. Many clients who engage in annual exclusion gifting ultimately cut back on those gifts over time because of fear of running out of money. This can cause stress on family members who have grown accustomed to receiving the gift regularly and planned it in their budgets. Even with the understanding that it is a gift, it is easy for people to expect it once it happens repeatedly. When the gift stops showing up, often without warning, there can be unexpressed anger, as no one wants to seem greedy or entitled. In reality, the receiver perhaps just needed to have the change communicated so that they could plan accordingly.

I strongly recommend that if you do choose to take advantage of the annual exclusion gifting option, do so in a way that ensures the recipients know that it is a gift and not to expect it from one year to the next. If you should find that you will not be gifting one year, let your recipients know in advance.

Techniques Applicable to All Wealth Categories

The first category of techniques applies to people in all wealth categories, though I'm not advocating your use of any one technique because I don't know your situation. Consult with and listen to an experienced estate planner who knows and understands your family's needs.

Severing Joint-Tenancy Arrangements

One of the most common and effective lifetime estate tax planning devices involves severing joint-tenancy arrangements. A joint tenancy is a form of property ownership in which at least two owners hold title to property as joint tenants with rights of survivorship, meaning that the last surviving joint tenant will become the full owner of the property.

People often enter joint-tenancy arrangements without really thinking or knowing about them. Quite often, someone else, such as a real estate title clerk, decides for them simply by typing the deed to reflect joint tenancy. The good thing about joint tenancy is that it is simple and at least avoids probate in the estate of the first joint tenant to die.

However, joint tenancy can ruin the estate planning of the first joint tenant to die by leaving that property to the surviving joint tenant. Since property automatically passes to the surviving joint tenant on the death of the first joint tenant, this is crucial to consider in estate planning for a blended family. This almost always means that the children and other loved ones of the deceased joint tenant will get nothing with respect to that property. This often conflicts with the intentions of the deceased joint tenant. What is in the deceased joint tenant's will, or worse yet, what the deceased joint tenant intended, is irrelevant.

The United States federal estate tax consequences of a joint tenancy differ depending on the identity of the joint tenants. If a husband and wife are the joint tenants, then there will be no federal estate tax for that property on the death of the first joint tenant because of the unlimited marital deduction. However, if anyone but spouses are joint tenants (e.g., a parent and a child or two unmarried partners), the federal estate tax consequences depend on who actually paid for the property. Consider this example: Unmarried partners are joint tenants on property that one of them actually paid for in total. At the death of the one who bought the property, the value of the property will be included in the person's estate who purchased the property.

I almost never recommend that couples, particularly those in blended-family relationships, own property as joint tenants. An estate planner who represents both partners may have an ethical or a prickly client relation problem by recommending severance of a joint-tenancy arrangement. This is because joint tenancy may work in favor of a younger partner, particularly one who is less wealthy than the other partner, because the younger partner is more likely to survive and receive that property. This causes a potential conflict between the partners. Nevertheless, I always recommend severance, reasoning that since you never really know who will survive, the parties are in the same boat at the time of the severance.

The beauty of severing a joint tenancy is that one partner can do it unilaterally without the other partner having to approve the change or even having to know about it. Again, this is a reason for separate representation, as a lawyer may be hamstrung by ethical obligations to the other partner and unable to participate in severance without telling the other partner if the lawyer represents both of you (except in the circumstance where the lawyer represents each of you separately).

This secrecy might be a signal that your partnership is not as solid as you'd like. You may want to ask yourself what it is that has you feeling the need to act in secret. Perhaps it is justified because your partner was asked and is being unreasonable. If that is how you see it, consider for a moment what you would feel if the situation were reversed. If you still believe you should go forward in secret, I strongly recommend you consider the ramifications of your partner finding out that you've gone behind his or her back—especially since he or she could be reading this book as well and considering the same thing.

I used to ask clients who are leaning toward being secretive to consider their compelling reason why. I used to have them articulate what is motivating them and what they hope to accomplish by making that choice. It often involves a decision that the client either is going to make or has made that his or her partner either will not like or will be hurt by. It might also involve an embarrassing fact that the client hasn't yet told his or her partner, such as the existence of a child unknown to his or her partner. I also had them look at other options and scenarios to open new possibilities.

Life insurance

Life insurance[46] policies can be owned by the insured or someone who has an "insurable interest" in the insured, such as a spouse, child, or business partner. Strangers can't insurance you. Life insurance can be community property or separate property. Life insurance policies can be obtained and owned by a trustee and held in trust for the benefit of beneficiaries who have an insurable interest in you.

There are several ways to distinguish between life insurance policy types. However, every type of life insurance is either whole life or term, or a mix between the two, despite the many different marketing names that insurance companies give life insurance policies, such as variable life or variable universal life.

In a whole life policy, a life insurance policy has a level premium that an insurance company cannot ever increase, no matter how long the insured lives. A term insurance policy has an annual premium that increases every year until the insured's death. Why? Because it is more likely that you will die with each passing year.

Life insurance can be a very valuable and flexible asset for use in the blended family, but it is not without its disadvantages and traps for the unwary. Unlike annuities, which are a bet to live, life insurance is a *bet to die*. In other words, the sooner that an insured dies, the less costly the life insurance. Unfortunately, the flip side also is true: the longer that the insured lives, the more expensive life insurance becomes.

One of the biggest advantages of life insurance is that it provides an immediate benefit on the death of one or two people. Life insurance provides cash, arguably the most flexible asset, at a time when it is often most needed. For example, a father in a blended family could provide an immediate inheritance

---

[46] There are many books about life insurance, so this discussion will be limited to the uses of life insurance in estate planning for blended families.

outright or in trust for the benefit of his children so that they would not have to wait until their mother's death to receive a significant inheritance.

This could dissuade the father's children from harassing the surviving stepmother for money or for acting as executor or successor trustee. In another example, life insurance could be used to provide a surviving stepfather with an income stream, allowing a mother to leave an income-producing asset (e.g., a family business) to her children.

Life insurance is not without its disadvantages. Chief among these disadvantages is the cost of maintaining life insurance until the insured's death, particularly if the insured lives well into old age. Many forms of life insurance increase exponentially in price as the insured approaches projected actuarial life expectancy age, increasing even more as the insured lives past projected life expectancy. There also is the disadvantage of potentially subjecting the life insurance to estate taxation if the insured either owns or controls the life insurance policy at death, although the insurance could be put into a properly structured life insurance trust to avoid this result.

There are many ways to categorize life insurance. However, for these purposes, I will divide life insurance into two types: single-life coverage (i.e., a policy on only one life) and joint-life coverage (i.e., a policy on two lives such as second-to-die or survivorship coverage).

Single-life coverage, whether it is whole life or term insurance, can be helpful in estate planning for blended families in many ways. Perhaps a father has minor children or a child with a disability for whom he needs to provide. Suppose that a partner wants to leave a valuable home to his surviving partner that comprises a large part of his estate, but also wants to leave a significant inheritance to his children from a prior union. Life insurance could be used to provide the children with a significant inheritance while allowing him to give the home to his partner.

Life insurance also could be used to create a stream of income for a surviving partner, while passing on other property (e.g., a family business, family homestead, or farm) to the children of the prior union. For blended couples who have their own children together (i.e., "ours"), life insurance could provide for the education and support of joint children, who are younger than the separate children of each partner.

Second-to-die life insurance is typically used to pay for coverage to assist in the payment of federal estate taxes where those taxes are deferred until the surviving partner's death through the federal estate tax marital deduction;

although, it is important to note that this marital deduction is only applicable to married partners. In second-to-die life insurance, partners are not the beneficiaries; the children or a life insurance trust usually are.

In estate planning for blended families, a properly structured second-to-die life insurance policy can assist paying the estate tax not only on the surviving partner's estate, but also on the amount of estate tax deferred from the estate of the first partner to die through the marital deduction, at least in estates of married partners.

Second-to-die life insurance is not without its problems, although many of these problems can be substantially reduced by a carefully crafted policy from a solid life insurance company. Second-to-die life insurance is often suggested when only one partner is insurable. However, this often isn't a good idea because that insurance can be more expensive than a single-life policy on the insurable partner.

Moreover, if the premium on a second-to-die life insurance policy is designed around the federal gift tax annual exclusion ($15,000 in 2021), there usually is a problem at the death of the first partner because the deceased partner loses his or her federal gift tax annual exclusion gift right at death. This usually means that the surviving partner will have to supply all the premiums with only one set of annual exclusion gifts, which requires the surviving partner to use his or her lifetime gift tax exemption, and when that is exhausted, start paying gift taxes. In a blended-family situation, a surviving partner who has children of his or her own may balk at essentially giving the children of the deceased partner annual exclusion gifts to pay the annual premiums or paying gift tax for the privilege of making gifts to his or her stepchildren. As you can well imagine, that typically doesn't go over very well and therefore usually doesn't happen.

For example, suppose partners purchase second-to-die life insurance, naming their separate children as the beneficiaries. Suppose further that the life insurance premiums are large enough to require use of both partners' annual exclusions. On the death of the first partner, the life insurance premiums almost always continue until the surviving partner's death, a financial burden usually borne by the surviving partner. Therefore, it might be advisable to create an arrangement with assets set aside to generate enough cash flow to pay the premiums for the remainder of the surviving partner's life. A single-life insurance policy on each partner's life, or a rider on a second-to-die life insurance policy that pays a benefit at the first death, should be considered.

Understand the benefits and drawbacks to life insurance before making your decision.

Annuities

By annuities, I mean contracts sold by life insurance companies. This is distinguished from private annuities, which are between individuals. This discussion is limited to the use of annuities in estate planning for blended families, as annuities can be quite complex with many features. Annuities are the opposite of life insurance and essentially are a "bet to live" because the issuer of the annuity, a life insurance company, bears the risk of the annuitant living too long. Annuities can provide protection against someone running out of money in old age because most annuities provide lifetime benefits.

In practice, I rarely recommended that wealthier people consider annuities because of the severe limitations it has on the estate planning. There is also a major income tax issue with variable annuities in that they essentially trade lower capital gains rates for higher regular income tax rates.

However, annuities can play a part in estate planning for blended families. For example, a wealthier partner could buy a lifetime annuity for her husband that could ensure him an income stream. However, there are other more tax-advantaged alternatives such as private unitrusts, direct gifts, bequests, or lifetime Qualified Terminable Interest Property (QTIP), all of which are discussed later in this book.

Opportunity shifts

One of the best lifetime estate planning techniques is called an opportunity shift, which has the benefit of never having the asset in your estate taxed in the first place. Opportunity shifts require either having an idea that will result in a very valuable asset in the future or having an asset that is not worth much now but is expected to significantly appreciate in the future. The technique involves transferring the asset or idea to people or a trust for the benefit of family members before it appreciates in value.

From the standpoint of blended families, opportunity shifts present chances to favor either children of the union, separate children, or both sets of children. This is a technique that should be used by someone who is very confident that the wealth he or she already has will be sufficient for his or her lifetime before he or she passes on an opportunity to increase his or her wealth.

For example, suppose that Mary Ann owns a piece of undeveloped real estate that is worth $1,000 per acre because it was only being used for pasture. However, the property will probably be developable into subdivisions in the future worth $25,000 per acre. Before development reaches her property, Mary Ann could transfer the property into a trust for her grandchildren at the lower value. The trust can then develop the property at the appropriate time and reap the benefits.

Charitable gift annuities

A charitable gift annuity is a simple one-to-two-page contract with a qualified charitable organization and is an unsecured promise made by a charity to pay a specified set amount each year to a person, who is called the "annuitant," in exchange for the annuitant contributing property to the charity. The payments to the annuitant depend solely on the age of the annuitant, and the payments are always higher the older an annuitant is when the charitable gift annuity begins. These annuity payments can begin immediately on transfer of the property, or they can be deferred to some point in the future.

While any property can be exchanged for a charitable gift annuity, cash is best because contributing appreciated property can create income tax on the capital gain (delta between the fair market value of the contributed property and the donor's adjusted income tax basis in the contributed property, which is recognized over the donor's remaining life expectancy). Since a charitable gift annuity can't be secured by any property of the charity, you should only enter into a charitable gift annuity with a large, financially strong charity. This is because the charity will not pay what a life insurance company would pay for a commercial annuity. On the death of the annuitant, the charity keeps the remainder of the property, making charitable intent so important. There aren't any particular blended-family considerations for a charitable gift annuity.

Below-market loans

At first blush, a loan might not appear to be an estate planning technique at all. However, if the loan can be made at a favorable interest rate (e.g., a below-market interest rate), this can be a very effective estate planning technique. This is especially true if the borrower can invest the loan proceeds to earn more than the interest to be paid on the loan, which would result in a gift-tax-free transfer of wealth. Below-market loans can be a very effective way to transfer wealth free from gift taxes.

Strategies for Wealth of More Than $1,000,000

In this section, I'll consider some lifetime estate planning techniques for those who have more than $1,000,000 in assets.

Life insurance trusts

A life insurance trust is an irrevocable trust, first and foremost. Once you form a life insurance trust, you usually can't get the policy (or the premiums paid) back from the trust. A life insurance trust involves either the transfer of an existing life insurance policy to a trust or the purchase of a new life insurance policy by a trust. Typically, life insurance premiums are paid through gifts to the life insurance trust, which are hopefully covered by annual exclusion.

One primary benefit of a life insurance trust is that, if properly structured, it keeps the insurance proceeds out of your estate for federal estate tax purposes. Ordinarily, when you own or control a life insurance policy, with the right to change beneficiaries or borrow against the policy, the proceeds are taxable in your estate for federal estate tax purposes, which could be catastrophic and a possible waste of the insurance proceeds. However, a life insurance trust can save those proceeds from estate taxation.

A life insurance trust assists in the payment of estate expenses and estate taxes either by loaning funds to your estate or by purchasing assets from your estate. It is imperative that the trustee not be obligated to lend money to your estate or to buy assets from your estate, as it would cause your policy to be subject to federal estate taxes.

For the majority who don't have to worry about the federal estate tax, a life insurance trust is a wonderful way to preserve life insurance proceeds for beneficiaries and to get independent management of the trust funds. Therefore, the reasons for protecting beneficiaries and providing income to them over time, as opposed to a lump sum, are far more important than keeping insurance proceeds out of an estate for federal estate tax purposes.

In blended families, life insurance trusts can be very useful, even for nontaxable estates. For example, a life insurance trust can be arranged to create an income stream for a surviving partner, with the principal going to the insured's children at the surviving partner's death. Likewise, a life insurance trust can be used to leave a significant sum to your children, freeing you to take care of your partner with your other property. It is critical that you select a third party as a trustee of a life insurance trust, especially for blended families.

Many blended-family clients begin the process believing that they can appoint a child from each of them as co-trustees, but I strongly advise against this, unless those two children have worked well together in the past. Usually, a financial institution will decline to serve as trustee of a trust that holds nothing but a life insurance policy (although a financial institution may agree to serve after the insured's death if the policy is large enough to satisfy the bank's minimum requirements), so you'll have to find a suitable third-party trustee.

Preferably, this unrelated third party will have no bias against your children or your partner. Again, neither of you, nor your children or even siblings, should serve as trustee of a life insurance trust that holds a life insurance policy on either you or your partner. However, if you insist on having family members or a partner serve as trustee of a life insurance trust, you should work with a competent estate planner to carefully spell out governance provisions, including tiebreaker provisions if you have more than one trustee, and select successor trustees.

Successor trustees are even more important when a partner insists on serving as a trustee because a desire to serve as trustee (or as executor) often declines when the surviving partner is attacked for his or her actions as executor or successor trustee, and when we get older, we may not want to put up with the same hassles as before. In my experience, the likelihood of beneficiaries complaining about the trustee is much higher in a blended family.

It is important to spend time on this part of the estate planning process. Your estate plan is only as good as the people in which you hire to implement. In my opinion, your selection of fiduciaries (e.g., trustee, executor, personal representative, conservator) is probably the most important aspect of estate planning, especially for blended families, and woefully too little time is usually spent on this part.

Annual exclusion gifts

Annual exclusion gifts remain one of the most tax-efficient ways to pass on wealth. The annual exclusion amount is issued annually by the Internal Revenue Service (IRS) and is based on inflation. In 2021, each person may gift up to $15,000 per year to an unlimited number of recipients.

These gifts must be of a "present interest," which, as a practical matter, means that they must either be made directly to the recipient or to a trust with as a "Crummey" (named after a famous 1968 court decision) clause in it. However, the rules are different and much tighter for annual exclusion gifts to grandchildren in trust. (I'm fond of saying to clients that "Crummey wasn't crummy"!)

A Crummey clause must give a trust beneficiary the unfettered right to withdraw the gift for a stated period (e.g., thirty days), meaning that a beneficiary could easily spoil a plan by withdrawing a gift. However, exercise of a Crummey right of withdrawal rarely happens for a whole host of possible reasons, but often because of the veiled but unstated threat to stop making gifts if the beneficiary exercises the withdrawal right.

In blended families, annual exclusion gifts can be used for a variety of reasons. For example, annual exclusion gifts can be used to fund life insurance premiums on the life of a parent or on the lives of the partners. If it is a single-life policy, it can either be owned by a trust for the benefit of the insured partner's children or outright by those children. However, if it is a second-to-die insurance policy insuring the lives of both partners, it should be owned and held by a carefully crafted trust arranged in such a way that the insurance is not included in the estate of either partner.

Much of annual exclusion gifting is inappropriate and ill-advised. A common example of inappropriate annual exclusion gifting occurs when clients make systematic annual exclusion gifts of income-producing property, such as interests in a family company, yet continue to receive income attributed to the gifted property that is neither reduced nor substantially affected by the gift. This most often happens when clients make gifts of interests in closely held businesses and continue to receive salary or rent or other forms of consideration from those businesses.

If a sales opportunity for the business materializes down the road, the senior generation may look adversely at the opportunity, even when the offered price is more than fair (or even generous). This could happen if the senior generation's share of the offer price would be insufficient (due to prior lifetime transfers) to generate the income that the senior generation presently enjoys through the salary and other perks. The junior generation may pass on the sales opportunity, despite the favorable offer, to maintain family peace.

There are often unaddressed and unspoken emotional components related to this sort of "gifting" where ownership occurs without power or control, and yet there is liability. When the gift is given this way, and the recipient has no say, choice, or buy-in, this can also create resentment and challenges down the road. No one wants to appear ungrateful, so often your heirs' feelings, thoughts, and concerns go unexpressed, potentially causing parents and their children to become less connected and more estranged over time.

If this is a strategy you are intending to use to mitigate estate taxes, see what you can do to include your beneficiaries in the decision making, so they know that their input and feelings matter. You'll be much more likely to have buy-in, and when situations arise, there's also a precedent for being able to talk things through together and hear all points of view before making final decisions.

Another common example of inappropriate lifetime giving occurs when life insurance premiums on a second-to-die life insurance policy are tied to annual exclusion gifts from both partners in a union. When one partner dies, that deceased partner can no longer make annual exclusion gifts, yet the policy has not paid off yet because the surviving partner is still alive. The choices are to use part of the survivor's lifetime applicable exclusion amount to supplement that partner's annual exclusion gifts, or start paying gift tax because the survivor has already exhausted his or her lifetime applicable exclusion amount, or reduce the policy coverage.

There are numerous other examples too, including the gifting of hard-to-value assets that require annual valuations as annual exclusion gifts, or where a client isn't likely to have a taxable estate in the first place!

Unlimited direct payments to qualified educational institutions and qualified health-care providers

Unlimited direct payments to qualified educational institutions and qualified health-care providers is one way to receive one of the biggest gift tax breaks in the Internal Revenue Code. The provision allows for unlimited direct payments of tuition and other educational expenses to qualified educational institutions and direct payment of health-care expenses, including health-insurance premiums paid to an insurance company, to qualified health-care providers.

In blended families, as in single-union families, this too often forgotten technique can be used to pay educational and health-care expenses for children older than eighteen and for grandchildren. In blended families, this provision can come in handy to assist stepchildren and step-grandchildren, too in their education or medical expenses.

Charitable remainder trusts

Charitable remainder trusts come in two varieties: charitable remainder annuity trust (CRAT) and the charitable remainder unitrust (CRUT). A CRAT is a creature of tax law, and it is a specially designed trust that can be created during lifetime or at death in a will. In a CRAT, you can retain a right to a set amount (but not less than 5 percent of the initial value of the property put into the CRAT) as an annuity payment, payable at least annually. Conversely, you can also create a CRAT for the benefit of others, such as children. A CRAT can be established for lifetime or a term that can't exceed twenty years. One or more qualified charities must be the final principal beneficiary of a CRAT. You can reserve the right to change the identity of the qualified charities that are also the final principal beneficiaries.

A CRUT is also a specially designed trust, similar to a CRAT. In a CRUT, one gives or retains a unitrust interest of not less than 5 percent of the value of the CRUT, which must be determined annually, with one or more qualified charities as final principal beneficiaries. The difference between the CRAT and the CRUT is that the payment is fixed at the start in the CRAT, meaning that the payment can neither go up nor go down during the CRAT term. Conversely, the CRUT payment is based solely on the value of the property. Therefore, the CRUT payout can either go up (if the value of the property in the CRUT increases) or down (if the value of the CRUT property declines in value). You can create a CRUT for the benefit of one or both partners or for others.

Suppose you want to give $100,000 to a charitable remainder trust and retain a lifetime right to 5 percent of the trust per year. Would you choose a CRAT or CRUT? In a CRAT, your annual payment would be set at $5,000 and would last until your death or until the CRAT runs out of money, whichever comes first. However, in a CRUT, your payment would be tied to the annual value of the CRUT property, meaning that if the property increased in value, your payment would increase, and vice versa.

Ordinarily, I recommend that younger people use a CRUT so that the value of the payments do not erode over time due to factors such as inflation. Now, this doesn't always mean that older folks should automatically opt for the CRAT; it is just one factor to consider. Also consider the type of property that the charitable remainder trust is expected to hold, because if the charitable remainder trust is expected to hold hard-to-value assets, a CRUT would have an annual appraisal of that property, which could get expensive.

If created during your lifetime, a charitable remainder trust can give you, as the donor, an income tax deduction. The amount of the deduction is a function of the term of the trust, the size of the retained interests of the income beneficiaries, the frequency of the payout and the applicable IRS interest rate in effect at the time of creation of the charitable remainder trust. The greater the size of the interest of the income beneficiary, the lesser the charitable deduction will be, and vice versa. But whether a charitable remainder trust yields an income tax deduction is a secondary consideration to the requirement that the prospective donor be significantly charitably inclined. Charitable intent is paramount in considering whether to enter a charitable planning technique because charity will receive a significant gift in any such technique, irrespective of how it is illustrated, which may upset children and other loved ones.

A charitable remainder trust is only appropriate where you are comfortable with a charity ultimately receiving the property. In a blended family, the beneficiary of the CRAT or CRUT could be a partner with lesser wealth, or it could be the children.

Do you know the difference between a CRAT and a CRUT?

Gift splitting

It is not unusual for one partner to have significantly more wealth than the other partner. Through gift splitting, the wealthier partner could make gifts of the entire amount, but, for gift tax purposes, it will be as if both partners made the gifts.[47]

Consider the following example: Nancy and Tom have been married for a few years. Nancy has significantly more wealth than Tom and wants to make

---

[47] Note: This technique only works if the partners are married.

annual exclusion gifts of $15,000 to each of her three children. Through gift splitting, which requires Tom's cooperation but no cost, Nancy could give each child $30,000. This requires the filing of a federal gift tax return. Now, if Nancy wanted to make larger lifetime gifts to her children, Tom could join in and double the amount of the gift as well.

However, in this instance, Tom would have to use part or all his gift tax applicable exclusion amount, which he may not want to do, especially if he has heirs of his own. It also may be appropriate to reimburse Tom for the loss of all or a part of his lifetime gift tax applicable exclusion amount because if his estate is taxable, his heirs will have to pay more tax because of this loss.

Private unitrusts

A private unitrust is a technique where, instead of giving the income beneficiary rights to the trust income, the beneficiary is given a right to a set percentage of the value of the trust, determined annually. The primary benefit of a private unitrust is that it eliminates (or at least minimizes) the potential for bickering between the income beneficiaries. Typically, income beneficiaries want assets invested to generate the most income, even at the expense of asset appreciation, as opposed to principal beneficiaries, who always want the assets invested for growth, even at the expense of immediate trust income. A private unitrust allows the trustee, who is caught in the middle, to invest for growth since it helps both the income and principal beneficiaries.

Private unitrusts work very well in blended families, especially where the income beneficiary is one of the partners, and the principal beneficiaries are the children of the other partner. Caution: If the partners are married and live in the United States, a private unitrust will not qualify for a marital deduction unless the spouse beneficiary is given the right to the greater of the unitrust percentage or the trust income. However, a marital deduction will not be important in every situation. Your professional advisor can assist you with this consideration.

Strategies for Those Worth More Than $5,000,000

In this section, I consider estate planning techniques available to persons who have more than $5,000,000 in wealth.

Private annuities

The private annuity is a very simple technique. It is a contract between someone who contributes property, called the "annuitant," to the other, in exchange for an unsecured (and that is very important) promise by the recipient to make lifetime payments to the annuitant. The private annuity comes in two basic varieties: a single-life annuity, in which annuity payments cease on the annuitant's death, and a joint and survivor annuity, in which annuity payments continue until the surviving annuitant's death.

The best assets for a private annuity are those that produce income or cash flow and are expected to appreciate in value. Some asset types, like depreciable property such as rental real estate, are disfavored for the private annuity because of the recapture of depreciation and investment tax credits that occur on creation of the private annuity.

For blended families, private annuity transactions are almost always of joint and survivor private annuities. However, a potentially difficult dynamic can often arise when the contributing annuitant's children by a prior union are the recipients of private annuity property. Depending on the relationship between your separate children with your surviving partner, a private annuity may not be the optimal plan because the surviving partner will be dependent on their stepchildren for annuity payments and for the prudent management of the property. There can be significant immediate adverse income tax consequences in the creation of a private annuity with certain types of property, so I strongly advise the assistance of a competent estate planner when creating private annuity.

Qualified Personal Residence Trust (QPRT)

A qualified personal residence trust (QPRT) is purely a creature of federal tax law. In a QPRT, a person puts the ownership of his or her home (either be a primary residence or be a second home) into a specially drafted trust, and he or she retains a right to live in the home for a certain period of time (e.g., ten years). At the end of the QPRT term, the donor must vacate the home or start paying fair market value rent to the trust or directly to the former beneficiaries of the trust, usually the children. Many people don't want to pay rent to remain in what they feel is their home. However, the home doesn't belong to them any longer at the end of the term; it belongs to the QPRT.

The benefit of a QPRT is it allows someone to make a discounted gift of his or her residence and thereby help reduce federal estate taxes. That benefit depends on the age of the owner and the number of years the owner reserves to stay in the home. The fact is the greater the period someone retains the right to live in the home, the higher the discount of the gift. However, the big downside of a QPRT is that if the donor doesn't survive the retained period of years, the transaction is essentially ignored for federal estate tax purposes, and the value of the home as of the donor's death will be included in the donor's estate for federal estate tax purposes.

In a blended-family situation, it is frequently the case that the partners reside in a home that belongs to only one partner. These usually aren't good candidates for a QPRT because the other partner may lack the resources either to find suitable housing if the owner/partner dies during the term of the QPRT or to pay market rate rent to the owner/partner's children. There may well be no poorer situation than to have to rent from stepchildren, who also could sell the house, not to mention the potential difficulties with determining fair market value rent.

I don't recall ever advising a blended-family couple to use a QPRT because of these potential problems. If the couple owns the home together but only one partner has children, the childless partner may object to leaving his or her share to his or her partner's children. If the couple owns the home together and each has children of a prior union, it may be difficult to leave the home to both sets of children unless there is a third-party trustee (which is unlikely since the only asset that a QPRT can own is a home) because these sets of children may not even know each other or work well together.

If only one partner owns the home but wants his or her partner to be able to reside in the property for life rent free, the QPRT will not accomplish this result because fair market value rent will have to be paid after the QPRT term. Again, making a surviving partner a tenant to your children is usually a bad idea. The QPRT might work for a blended couple with children together, if those children are the sole remainder beneficiaries, as that would be akin to a QPRT for any family.

Family limited entities

Family limited partnerships and family limited liability companies have existed for a very long time. In a family entity, typically the parents of the children create the family entity and contribute property in exchange for interests. The principal sought after gift or estate tax benefit is the ability to give away discounted interests in the family entity while retaining control. The facts concerning the creation of the family entity are critical to its success. Therefore, I strongly advise that you not form a family entity without competent professional advice.

In blended families, I rarely advised clients to form family entities where there would be a mixing of children from both partners, unless the children are comfortable being partners with each other have demonstrated some degree of competence in owning and managing something together already.

Some parents with the means to do so will create a family foundation to give all the children in their lives (whatever their ages) a chance to work together and build competence. If the parents continue to run the show and wield most of the power, then their initial intention is lost, and the children do not get the chance to truly see what they can accomplish together (or to determine without a doubt that they cannot work together). Again, it is important to communicate with your children for their input and buy-in prior to setting up an entity ostensibly to have them work together.

Otherwise, they may feel put-upon or forced, and while you probably won't hear about it (as they will not want to appear ungrateful), they may have resentment that can surface at the time of your death. In partners that also have children together, the same admonition applies. An occurrence I see too often in blended families is that in this scenario, the "ours" children frequently are shunned by both sets of separate children, who see their half-siblings as treated differently, and there is perceived favoritism.

Strategies for Those Who Worth More Than $15,000,000

Finally, in this section, I consider estate planning techniques that should be considered by persons who possess more than $15,000,000 in wealth.

Large gifts, including defined value gifts

Where appropriate, making gifts during your lifetime of amounts larger than the available annual exclusion can be the most powerful estate planning move, especially if the donor is able to transfer the wealth through more than one generation (i.e., to grandchildren or beyond). Use of the applicable exclusion amount during lifetime gets the future income and appreciation in value of that gifted property out of your estate. (Larger gifts tend to be made in trust.) It is less expensive to give property away during your lifetime than it is to die with that property due to the way gift tax is computed and paid. The recipient does not have to pay the federal gift tax but is responsible for the recipient's share of the federal estate tax.

Consider the following example: Assume that Alice is worth $25,000,000 and that she has $5,000,000 applicable exclusion amount remaining, and a 40 percent federal estate and gift tax rate. Alice would like to give $10,000,000 to a child and asks whether she should give it away during her lifetime or wait until her death. If Alice gives the $10,000,000 to her child during her lifetime, she'll have to pay $2,000,000 in federal gift tax, but her child gets the whole $10,000,000 because Alice must pay the gift tax out of her remaining $15,000,000.

If, instead, Alice died with a $25,000,000 estate, she would owe $10,000,000 in federal estate tax after using her $5,000,000 exemption ($20,000,000 times 35 percent). The $10,000,000 bequest to her child pays for that child's share of federal estate tax. This means that the child would receive a net $6,500,000, since the estate tax on the $10,000,000 is $3,500,000. As you can see, the child comes out much better in the lifetime gift situation as long as the child doesn't need to sell the gifted property, as the child takes the parent's income tax basis (usually the original cost of the gifted property). If you are interested in this type of situation, discuss it with your tax advisor.

Unfortunately, the costs of lifetime giving can be significant. For starters, neither the property nor its future income or appreciation is available to the donor after the gift. It is not unusual for a partner to object to the other partner making such a large gift, and I see this as a much more common objection in blended families.

Secondly, the recipients of a gift of property take the tax basis that you had in the property. For example, suppose you had a piece of real estate that you bought years ago for $100,000 that is now worth $1,000,000. You can give away this property to your children free of federal gift tax. However, if your children sold the property for $1,000,000, they would have $900,000 in taxable gain ($1,000,000 selling price minus $100,000 tax basis).

In blended families, assuming that the other partner is open to the idea even though it means that he or she would be deprived of the continuing use of, or access to income from the property to be gifted, a large gift to the giving partner's children can ensure that certain specific assets such as a family home or a family business stay in the partner's biological family.

A defined value gift is one where you can state (usually by formula, but it can be a fixed number) how much is to be given. For example, it may be that you want to make a gift of your remaining applicable exclusion amount, and no more. People use defined value gifts in situations in which they are giving property that is hard to value, such as land or interests in a family business. It is extremely important that the lawyer who drafts a defined value gift knows how to draft one. It is also critical that a defined value gift be consistently reported as such on the federal gift tax return. I strongly advise that you hire a qualified tax professional to prepare a gift and income tax return for a defined value gift.

Equalization of estates

When there is a large disparity in wealth between partners, there can be an estate planning advantage to having the wealthier partner make a large, tax-free gift to the other partner of an amount that equalizes the partners' estates by value. This was more common when the federal estate taxable brackets ranged from 37 to 55 percent, which is no longer the case.

If the federal estate tax is "flat" (in other words, very little spread between the highest and lowest federal estate tax rates, as has been the case for several years), equalization makes little sense, except in giving the poorer partner enough property to use his or her estate tax exemption. This technique should only be considered by couples who have been together for a long time and who have a solid relationship; the giving partner can't get his or her wealth back if the couple subsequently splits. I rarely ever mentioned this technique to blended-family couples because of the high rate of separation among these couples.

Lifetime Qualified Terminable Interest Property (QTIP)

The Lifetime Qualified Terminable Interest Property (QTIP) trust is an irrevocable trust that you create during your lifetime. Irrevocable means exactly that: it's permanent, even if the couple separates, which can be a drawback, particularly in blended-family relationships where the incidence of separation exceeds even the high rate of first marriage divorces.[48]

Don't confuse a QPRT and a QTIP.

I often worked with couples where one partner didn't have enough wealth to use up the estate tax applicable exclusion amount if that partner died first, while the other partner had significant wealth and a taxable estate. While the wealthier partner would like to save his or her heirs some estate tax, he or she will usually object to simply giving the other partner significant wealth to equalize the estates. This is much truer in blended-family relationships.

There are several requirements for a lifetime QTIP trust. The other partner must be given all the trust income for that partner's lifetime, even if they divorce. It also requires the filing of a gift tax return and a special election on that return to be timely filed. For these reasons, lifetime QTIP trusts should only be considered by spouses who have a long-term, solid relationship.

However, the lifetime QTIP trust can be designed to cause wealth to be taxed in the other partner's estate, thereby using up that other partner's estate tax applicable exclusion amount while allowing the wealthier partner to control where that property goes after the other partner's death. This technique could save a significant amount of federal estate tax for the wealthier partner's heirs and is particularly popular in married blended-family relationships.

Grantor Retained Annuity Trust (GRAT)

The Grantor Retained Annuity Trust (GRAT) is another creature of federal tax law. In a GRAT, one creates a specially designed irrevocable trust with property and retains a right to an annuity from the trust for a specified period of time. A GRAT may only be created during one's lifetime. The retained annuity can be a flat annuity or can increase by as much as 20 percent per year. The benefit of a GRAT is that it allows you to discount the taxable gift by the actuarial value of your retained interest.

The longer the GRAT term, the greater the amount of the retained interest, and vice versa. The greater the amount of the retained interest, the lesser the amount of the taxable gift, and vice versa. If you survive the term of the GRAT, then your interest ceases, and you can't have any more interest in that property, which passes to the principal beneficiaries tax free. However, if you

---

[48] Note: The Lifetime QTIP technique is only available to married couples.

don't survive the term, the value of the property remaining in the GRAT will be taxed in your estate, which is the significant downside of the GRAT.

The issues with respect to the GRAT for blended families revolve around the identity of the remainder beneficiaries of the GRAT. In the typical blended-family GRAT, the children of the contributing partner are almost always the remainder beneficiaries. Blended couples who want to use this tool for both of their children from prior relationships are advised to set up two separate trusts so that the stepsiblings are not joint beneficiaries under one trust. Setting up separate "yours, mine, and ours" GRATs can work well if you communicate with your heirs in advance, and they understand the mechanism, amounts, and rationale in creating your plan this way.

Charitable lead trusts

Charitable lead trusts received a lot of publicity several years ago when Jacqueline Kennedy Onassis set up one in her will, which, ironically, never came into effect. A charitable lead trust is essentially the flipside of a charitable remainder trust. In a charitable lead trust, one or more charities receive the income interest, with one or more individuals receiving the remaining property at the end of the trust term. Like charitable remainder trusts, there are two basic forms of charitable lead trusts: charitable lead annuity trusts and charitable lead unitrusts. Charitable lead trusts can be formed during your lifetime or at death. Here, I'll focus on charitable lead trusts that can be set up during your lifetime.

There are two types of lifetime charitable lead trusts: a so-called grantor trust and a nongrantor trust. In a grantor charitable lead trust, the creator of the trust gets an income and gift tax charitable contribution deduction but must pay the income tax on all of the charitable lead trust's income. There are situations when the grantor variety works, such as when you have a large income year and don't foresee another one anytime soon.

In my experience, most lifetime charitable lead trusts are of the nongrantor variety. The creator of a nongrantor charitable lead trust gets a gift tax (but not income tax) charitable contribution deduction. However, the nongrantor charitable lead trust gets an unlimited income tax charitable contribution deduction for all amounts paid to the charitable beneficiaries.

The most important point about any charitable lead trust is that the ultimate recipients must be able to support themselves during the term of the charitable lead trust because they won't receive anything from the charitable lead trust until the end of the charitable lead trust term, which could go on for many years. Typically, the children (or more remote descendants) of the contributing partner are the remainder beneficiaries of a charitable lead trust.

Depending on the terms of the charitable lead trust, the property might be distributed directly to the remainder beneficiaries at the end of the charitable lead trust term or continue to be held in a regular trust. In blended families, if the charitable lead trust will distribute directly to beneficiaries, then children of the partners can be financially separated, which is usually a good thing.

Installment Sale to an Intentionally Defective Grantor Trust (IDGT)

In a technique called an installment sale to an Intentionally Defective Grantor Trust (IDGT), typically a parent sells property to an irrevocable trust in exchange for a promissory note that calls for installment payments. Beneficiaries of the trust are usually the parent's children or more remote descendants. There are several benefits when making a sale to an IDGT. Perhaps the biggest benefit is that a property that is expected to appreciate freezes the value of the seller's estate and passes on the appreciation free from estate or gift tax.

Some estate planning techniques are on the cutting edge, and there are uncertainties in the law pertaining to these estate planning techniques, which translates into greater risk. Sales to IDGTs fall into this category since there is some disagreement among estate planning commentators as to the income tax consequences, if any, of dying with an unpaid installment note after a sale to an IDGT. Nevertheless, there are many reasons to sell assets expected to appreciate in the future to an IDGT, usually in exchange for an installment note.

By "intentionally defective," I mean that the irrevocable trust is treated as owned by the creator of the trust for income tax, but not for estate tax purposes. There is nothing defective about the IDGT; it is purposely set up that way. The "intentionally defective" trust part of the technique is very safe from a tax standpoint since the Internal Revenue Code has mandated this result since 1924. Likewise, the ignored sale aspect is also safe as it is the official Internal Revenue Service (IRS) position. The big uncertainty is the tax consequences if the seller dies before the installment note is paid off. It is either a recognized gain or it isn't.

For blended families, sales to Intentionally Defective Grantor Trusts must be very carefully designed, even more so than for other families. The trustee of the purchasing irrevocable trust must be an independent third party because the beneficiaries might be children from both partners as well as possibly a surviving partner. This is where it will be imperative to coordinate the selection of an executor of the selling partner's estate (which will be a creditor until the note is paid off) with the selection of the trustee of the purchasing irrevocable trust so that there is no friction after the selling partner's death if the note is not paid off by then.

Guarantees

Like the low-interest loan, the guarantee of certain debts of children and other relatives can be a very effective estate planning technique if the borrowing children can earn more with the borrowed funds than the cost of the guarantee, if a guarantee fee is charged. If a guarantee fee is not charged, the extension of the guarantee may be treated as a gift for federal gift tax purposes.

However, guarantees can be very dangerous to the financial stability of the guaranteeing partner, especially if the borrowers default on their loans and the guaranteeing partner is called on by the lender to pay off the loans. Clients can go overboard with guarantees of the debts of children during profitable times and suffer significant financial reversals in the process. Caution is advised.

In blended families, guarantees must be even more carefully considered than usual because there might be resistance by one partner to a guaranteeing partner's guaranteeing debts of her children since this could impact financial security if the loan must be paid off by the guaranteeing partner. Moreover, coordination of selection of executors and successor trustees is critical because if the other partner is the successor trustee or executor, that partner may not cooperate with the guarantee, possibly resulting in litigation.

For example, suppose that Rhett guaranteed a debt for one of his boys, Rex, and then he dies. Rhett named Rex's stepmother, Scarlett, as executrix. Rex is unable to pay the debt, and the creditor calls for Rhett's estate to pay off the guarantee. Scarlett objected to Rhett guaranteeing Rex's debt when first decided. If she won't pay off the debt, she will force the creditor (and Rex) to sue Rhett's estate, which will result in legal fees, delays, and probably some hard feelings from Rex.

Action Steps

First and foremost, you will need to determine if lifetime estate planning is a viable option. Look at your current needs as well as your needs going forward that you are aware of, and contingencies you need to plan for (e.g., long-term care and estate taxes). You can work with your accountant or other estate planning advisors to determine figures that would more than take care of all your concern, so you know your level of freedom and play beyond those numbers.

If you determine that lifetime estate planning is a good option for you to consider, spend some quality time reviewing this chapter—make notes about what you could see for your family as a result. If you don't see one as a good idea, write down your reasons for that too. If it is purely a gut feeling, you may want to consider doing more research before jumping to a conclusion too quickly.

Once you get a sense for which plans seem the best options, it's time to do more research and determine which will be probable candidates and why. See if you can narrow down your choices even further. As you explore your options, keep a running list of questions to find answers to by researching on the Internet, asking credible sources, and reading relevant books. When you are ready to talk to your attorney and the clock is ticking for billable hours, you will have a clear direction and well-researched questions, which will streamline the whole process and get you the results you want expediently while minimizing costs.

Once you've made your determination about how you would like to implement the lifetime estate planning options, take time to connect with your beneficiaries prior to signing anything to make sure that what you're considering is in alignment with their values, lifestyle choices, and goals. You may learn about concerns they have that you had not considered, which may be more pressing than the ones you are addressing. You may learn that there's a great deal of discomfort around being included in a trust with stepsiblings and half-siblings, which may lead to discord and possible litigation down the road. Taking the time to do this part in a way that allows for the hopes and concerns of your intended beneficiaries to come out, could save a lot of unanticipated grief and upset (and it could save you money and time by keeping you from preparing documents that you end up not signing).

Testamentary Estate Planning

Introduction

Chapter 8 dealt with estate planning during your lifetime that takes effect immediately. This chapter concerns itself with estate planning that goes into effect at death. I address several issues that arise in testamentary planning and how these issues can impact blended-family estate planning.

I could also discuss topics such as postdeath challenges to marriage contracts or property agreements, but I have opted not to do so since these topics really aren't planning in its truest sense. Nevertheless, such postdeath challenges are always on the radar and should not be discounted.[49]

Testamentary estate planning for blended families requires patience and skill. There are a lot of ways to mitigate creating a mess for your loved ones after you are gone. Hopefully, the topics in this chapter will assist you in avoiding many of the obvious and not so obvious traps for the unwary.

In Terrorem Clauses

An in terrorem or "no contest" clause is placed in a will or a trust, and it can effectively prevent heirs or beneficiaries from disputing the terms of the will or

---

[49] With respect as to why estate plans can fail, see Chapter 7.

trust by taking away whatever they receive in the will or trust if they contest it in court. The purpose of these clauses is to reduce rancor and litigation in estates and trusts. These clauses don't always work, though, as they are very dependent on applicable state or provincial laws and the interpretation of each jurisdiction in court.

Your estate planning attorney should be able to tell you how these clauses fare in the courts of your state. In terrorem clauses are being used with increasing frequency, particularly in blended families. For example, your children may be at odds with your partner, and you may plan on leaving part of your estate to your children and part to your partner. Maybe the problem is that your children want it all.

An in terrorem clause could effectively preclude your children from challenging what you leave to your partner by forcing your children to surrender their inheritance if they mount a challenge to your estate plan. These clauses send a strong message to not mess with what you want to have happen with your estate.

Communicating your intention before you die and doing what you can to promote peace and reduce rancor will support the purpose of such a clause. If your children were to learn of this clause at the time of your death, without hearing or knowing your concerns, they may find other ways to make your partner's experience less than pleasant—even if they cannot go about it litigiously.

Looking at the current situation in your blended family, do you see a need for an in terrorem clause in your will? If so, take some time to write down your concerns and what you don't want to see happen that may end in needing an in terrorem clause. Be prepared to share this decision with all your family members preferably while you are alive so that everyone understands what led you to this decision and what your hopes are as a result.

Disinheriting Family

Of course, some situations call for more drastic action. An in terrorem clause won't help in a situation where you wish, for example, to leave nothing to a particular child of yours, because that child has nothing to lose by contesting your estate or trust.

There are many possible reasons why you might disinherit family members. For example, you may no longer have a relationship with a particular child. I run across the following scenarios repeatedly in blended families that bring forward a need for this sort of drastic measure:

- When a child vehemently objects to your choice of a partner and, therefore, rejects you as well.
- When a child has been a victim of parental alienation and has been conditioned to not have anything to do with you while being loyal to his or her other biological parent.
- When you have given a particular child a significant sum of money or property during your lifetime.

Whatever your reason, I believe that it is important to describe that reason in your will or trust. This allows you to tell your side of the story because when you are dead, you are unable to speak for yourself. I strongly encourage you to make attempts to communicate with that particular child during your lifetime to at least give him or her a chance to see the consequences of his or her choices while there's still a chance to rectify the breach in your relationship.

Is there anyone in your blended family that you plan on disinheriting? This would mean excluding him or her from any transfer of property, other assets, or monies. This is the time to have an open conversation about how you have come to this conclusion and your reasons. Is there anything that individual could say or do that would change your mind in the future? These are important areas to address in writing now, as memories change and so do people over time. If something were to happen to either of you tomorrow, what is it you would want that individual to know about why you've made this choice today, and what do you wish you could have seen happen in the future to change your mind?

One powerful exercise is to share what you enjoyed most about that person prior to when things went in a different direction. If it is a matter of having already been quite generous toward the person, take time to share what you've enjoyed about giving during your lifetime and witnessing what he or she chose to do as a result of receiving your generosity.

Communicating your reasons why you've made the choices you have will help to ease the blow and keep your memory focused in a positive direction.

Equalization of Estates

I rarely see partners in blended families wanting to equalize the sizes of their respective estates if one partner is far wealthier than the other partner, even if doing so would save estate tax. If this continues to be a source of conflict for you, there may be an underlying concern that is not getting addressed in other ways in the overall estate planning process. If attempts to communicate do not yield satisfying results, I highly recommend you consider working with a coach, facilitator, or other trained professional who can support you two at getting to the heart of the matter so that you can both feel good about your estate plan.

Powers of Appointment

A power of appointment is a tool contained in a trust intended to provide flexibility in estate planning after your death by giving someone a right, called a power of appointment, to shift trust property by appointing it between beneficiaries or to remove a beneficiary altogether. A power of appointment can be a dangerous thing because if it is unlimited, the holder of that power could effectively rewrite your estate plan.

Powers of appointment come in two varieties: A general power of appointment, where there are no limits on the ability of the power holder to appoint the property even if appointing the property for the benefit of her estate, and a limited or special power of appointment, where the power holder can't appoint the property to himself or to his estate but rather to or between the persons (or charities) that you name.

For example, you may leave your estate equally to your children, but give someone a power of appointment to shift property only between the children to account for postdeath changes in circumstances between the children. Suppose that one of your children has a significant medical need that arises after your death and your other children don't really need the money. In that situation, your power holder could simply shift trust property between your children to increase the share of the sick child.

There is a dark side to powers of appointment. This is why powers of appointment are sometimes referred to as a "power to disappoint." This dark side can rear its ugly head, particularly in blended families. For example, there could be acrimony between your partner and your children after your death. If you leave a significant part of your estate to your children but give your partner a general power of appointment, your partner could rewrite your estate plan after your death and even shift your property to his or her own children, which is rarely what people want.

For this reason, powers of appointment in blended families are almost always carefully crafted special or limited powers of appointment, particularly where the surviving partner is the one who is given the power of appointment. This is where the "power to disappoint" can "encourage" children to take care of their stepparent after you are gone.

Before using a power of appointment, consider the potential challenges your heirs will contend with as a result.

Now that you understand power of appointment, discuss as a couple the degree of flexibility you want your estate to have. This is an important decision, especially when you consider the ages of your children now and going forward as their needs and capacities will shift as they grow. Think about what you want for them and what you hope your estate would provide if you were to pass away unexpectedly today.

Would you want their access and support to shift based on benchmarks in their lives other than age (e.g., graduation, marriage, birth of first child)? Remember, you get to craft this how you want it. The more you think these it through and capture your thoughts in writing, the easier it will be to address your desires and questions when you work with your attorney to prepare the necessary documents.

Once you determine the degree of flexibility you want, you need to determine who will have that role and how much power you will give to the person. Whomever you choose, make sure you give him or her clear standards to work from, so that he or she knows what is involved in the role. This way he or she can feel guided by your wishes as he or she makes decisions on your behalf for the people you love.

Marital Deduction Transfers

This section only applies to married couples in blended-family relationships who worry about the federal estate tax. Unfortunately, given the uncertainty in the estate tax laws that will probably persist for the immediate future, even those who have relatively modest estates may have to worry about the federal estate tax.

There are several ways that a transfer to or for the benefit of a spouse can qualify for the federal estate tax marital deduction. In the following three scenarios, a straightforward and an obvious choice for a traditional, nuclear family becomes a bit more challenging for blended-family situations. (In the three scenarios, the surviving spouse is effectively the absolute owner or controller of the property.)

This is where the "yours, mine, and ours" scenario can cause a lot of concern and conflict, as each spouse tends to want to focus his or her attention and emphasis on the children that are biologically connected to him or her, and there is an underlying fear that the other spouse will likely treat differently, or exclude completely, the nonbiological children.

The first type of spousal transfer that qualifies for the marital deduction is a will or trust. In a direct bequest, all the property belongs to the surviving partner, who can do whatever he or she wants with it. In my experience, I don't see direct and outright transfers to a spouse very often in blended-family situations because the surviving recipient spouse, especially one who has children of his or her own, will probably not transfer the property at death to the children of the predeceased spouse at his or her death.

The second type of spousal transfer that qualifies is a transfer in trust for the benefit of the surviving spouse, together with giving that spouse a general power of appointment over the property in the trust. This means that the surviving spouse will be able to give that property to persons of his or her choosing. This doesn't often appeal to people in blended-family relationships, particularly where the recipient spouse has his or her own children from prior relationships. The surviving spouse can exercise the general power of appointment to give all the property to himself or herself, which blended families also usually don't want.

The third type of spousal transfer that qualifies for the federal estate tax marital deduction is the estate trust, where the recipient spouse has the benefit of all the trust property during his or her lifetime, and the property passes to the person of the recipient spouse's choosing at his or her death.

Again, I don't see this one very often in blended families either because the recipient spouse has the power to direct the trust property to persons of his or her own choosing. This means that there is no guarantee that the predeceased transferor spouse's children will receive the amount of the trust property originally desired since the surviving spouse is free to transfer that property at whatever levels to anyone he or she wants. The will or trust can give him or her rights to some principal as well.

So, is it three strikes and you're out? Or is there a way to get a marital deduction on a transfer for the benefit of the surviving spouse, yet dictate where the trust property goes when the surviving spouse dies? Yes—it is called a Qualified Terminable Interest Property (QTIP) trust.

Qualified Terminable Interest Property (QTIP)

The QTIP trust has several very strict requirements to qualify for the federal estate tax marital deduction. First, there must be a transfer in trust for the benefit of a spouse, which means the person to whom you are married. Second, the surviving spouse must be a US citizen.[50]

Third, the trust must provide that during the surviving spouse's lifetime, the only person who can receive any benefits (income or principal) from the trust is the surviving spouse. Fourth, the trust must require that the surviving spouse be given all the income from the trust at least annually. Finally, the executor of your estate (or the trustee of your living trust if you've used a living trust instead) must make an election on your federal estate tax return. If you fail any of these requirements, you lose the entire marital deduction, which subjects the trust to federal estate tax in the deceased spouse's estate.

What happens when the surviving spouse dies? The cost of making a QTIP election is that the value of the property over which the QTIP election was made, valued as of the date of the surviving spouse's death, is included in the surviving spouse's estate for federal estate tax purposes as if the surviving spouse owned the property at death.

The property is taxed in the surviving spouse's estate even though the surviving spouse has no control over the property and has no say so about who gets that property at the surviving spouse's death. This can have the effect of increasing the amount of estate tax that the surviving spouse's estate will owe, which can be unfair to the recipients of the surviving spouse's estate. This is

---

[50] There is a way that foreign spouses can receive a marital deduction, which is called a "qualified domestic trust," but the requirements are beyond the scope of this book.

why there is a provision of the Internal Revenue Code that permits the heirs of the surviving spouse's estate to collect the extra tax from the heirs of the estate of the first spouse to die.

The most important thing to know here is that the partners in blended families generally shouldn't waive the right of their estate to pursue the extra tax caused by the QTIP election since that share hasn't paid any estate tax on it.

Who should make the QTIP election?

The QTIP election must be made by the executor of the deceased spouse's estate, or the trustee of the deceased spouse's living trust on the deceased spouse's federal estate tax return, so the QTIP election is optional. The question becomes: Who should be the executor or trustee for the first spouse to die? Who should decide whether a QTIP election is made, understanding that the surviving spouse's estate could be adversely affected? The answer goes to the question of who should serve as executor or trustee of a partner in a blended-family relationship, since that person will make the call on a QTIP election. For many reasons, I believe it best for a disinterested third party to make the QTIP election.

A surviving spouse can be inclined to make the QTIP election because it puts off estate tax until the surviving spouse dies. This preserve the estate for the surviving spouse since the estate tax won't be paid, even if it increases estate tax in the surviving spouse's estate, especially since the property of the first spouse to die will be charged the extra estate tax. Likewise, the children of the first spouse to die might be inclined to not make a QTIP election if it reduces the overall amount of estate tax they'll have to pay. The problem that children have with the QTIP election is that once the election is made, they'll be liable for an estate tax on that property without any ability to reduce the estate tax through estate planning because the trustee is the owner of the subject property.

I believe that it is best for an independent third party to evaluate a situation and decide whether to make a QTIP election in the estate of the first spouse to die. Some of the factors to consider include the size projection of the surviving spouse's estate, the age differences between the spouses, the health of the surviving spouse, and the expected estate tax exemption.

Who should decide what assets fund the QTIP portion?

Again, the executor or trustee makes the decision as to the assets over which the QTIP election is made. The ultimate recipients of the estate of the first spouse to die will want those assets to be invested in high-income and low-appreciation investments (e.g., bonds) because they don't want to increase their estate tax liability when the stepparent dies.

The surviving spouse stepparent will want as much income as he or she can get, but he or she might not care whether the assets experience any growth unless he or she is young at the time of his or her spouse's death. However, his or her children will care a lot because they may have to pay estate tax on the appreciation that arises after their stepparent's death, especially since those children won't receive any of that appreciated property.

Should you waive pursuit of estate taxes from the recipients of a QTIP portion?

In single-marriage families where the beneficiaries of the estates are the same, it is common for the surviving spouse to waive the pursuit of the estate tax attributable to the QTIP property. However, in blended families, where the ultimate recipients of the spouses' individual estates are usually different people, this type of plan typically will not comport with the desires of most blended-family partners. I almost always recommend that blended-family partners not waive pursuit of federal estate tax.

Marital deductions and QTIP options

Are there any possible snags you see that need to be considered before deciding on these tax avoidance options? One thing to keep in mind is that most attorneys and accountants who do estate planning are focused on avoiding taxes and looking at "governance" issues (i.e., who will be the decision maker once you are no longer able to make decisions about your possessions and what will be done with them). They will need your guidance to consider other issues that are at stake related to your family's overall structure and differences in need.

Unitrust Option

There is a way to create a win-win for both groups of competing beneficiaries. If you have a partner as the income beneficiary (e.g., he or she has access to and benefits from the interest earned on the assets of the trust) and your children as principal beneficiaries (i.e., your children will receive the remaining assets in the trust at the time of the surviving spouse's death) in a traditional trust, the age-old conflict is how the trust is to be invested. Income beneficiaries want high income, which almost always can be achieved at the cost of growth in the value of the trust's assets. Principal beneficiaries want growth, which can generally be achieved only at the cost of income.

In a unitrust, you can give your partner an interest equal to a percentage of the fair market value of the trust annually for life or for a shorter period, which can be payable in monthly or quarterly installments, with your children being the principal beneficiaries. Your partner will benefit from the growth in the value of the trust's assets, as will your children as principal beneficiaries. Therefore, the assets can be invested for growth, and both sides will benefit from the growth, which should reduce the tension between traditional trust income and trust beneficiaries.

A client asked me to explain a reason why someone would choose not to go this route and use one of the other conventions mentioned. My response was that if you need a QTIP marital deduction, the spousal payout would have to be the greater of the trust's income or the unitrust amount. Additionally, if the trust assets need to be valued annually, it can get expensive to appraise assets such as real estate and closely held business assets.

Life Estates

A life estate is a mechanism where an owner of real estate transfers title to another person but retains the sole lifetime right to use the property. On the death of the original owner, called a "life tenant," the recipient becomes the full owner of the property. A life estate also can be used to transfer a life estate in your home to your partner and transfer the remainder interest to your children. Life estates can be viewed as a simpler alternative to a trust. You can transfer ownership while still retaining use of your property during your lifetime.

For several reasons, I don't generally like life estates for blended-family estate planning; I prefer trusts instead. For starters, your partner will be liable for real estate taxes and home repairs, and if he or she lacks the resources to pay these expenses, he or she won't be able to borrow money secured by a mortgage on the home without the consent of your beneficiaries. In blended families, given the greater likelihood of conflict between your children and your surviving partner, life estates can create more trouble than they are worth. Even if everyone is on good terms right now, I've seen enough instances where underlying resentments and past hurts that were never addressed with the parent who passes away come out against the surviving partner. Additionally, the property that is subject to the life estate is exposed to the creditors of the surviving partner and your children—a properly crafted trust can protect against that.

If you are considering a life estate to have fewer initial expenses than a trust, consider the potential future cost—both emotionally and financially—should family dynamics take a shift for the worse at one of your deaths. What may seem like a money saver now may in the future produce unnecessary suffering and discord that was never intended.

Charitable Lead Trusts

Most charitable lead trusts are created to become effective at death. Charitable lead trusts can be set up to "zero out" federal estate tax using a formula. Because heirs won't receive any benefits from a charitable lead trust until it terminates, they should be used only by those who have heirs who can afford to wait for their inheritance, possibly for a long time.[51]

Who Should Serve as Executor and Successor Trustee of a Living Trust?

Introduction

Now, I want to look at the role of trustee. In my view, a disinterested, third-party professional (which does not necessarily mean a bank or trust company)

---

[51] See Chapter 8 for more information about charitable lead trusts.

is the recommended option to serve as executor and successor trustee of a living trust in the majority of blended-family situations in order to reduce rancor between the heirs and to prevent possible shenanigans.

I know that this advice may not be taken well by your partner or your children, both of whom may certainly want the jobs. Unfortunately, the casebooks are littered with family upsets and litigation that wouldn't exist other than the fact that either children from a prior union or a surviving partner served in one of these fiduciary capacities.

Some of you will wonder if it would work to have your partner serve with a child from a prior union. In my experience, this rarely is successful and often creates more animosity and resentment, translating into higher costs, with the litigation lawyers being the big winners.

For those of you still attached to having a family member, or multiple family members, fulfill the roles of executor and successor trustee, there's much you can to do prepare them adequately and to allow them to determine if they are truly equipped to meet the requirements of the role and carry out the duties. You would be wise to include communication training and educational support to make sure that they are given every chance of success possible; it's a terrible position to be put in otherwise.

You may ask about a bank or trust company serving as executor, as trustee of trusts in a will, or as successor trustee of a living trust. For starters, while the banks and trust companies are professionals and generally do a competent job, there are many situations where they simply will not serve. There are a variety of reasons for this. For starters, the bank or trust company may not like the rules contained in the will or trust document under which it is expected to serve, making it important to have whatever bank or trust company review a draft of the document if you want a particular bank or trust company to serve.

Additionally, many banks and trust companies have minimum worth requirements for their service, so the value of the property going into the trust or estate may not be high enough for them to take the job. If you want a particular bank or trust company to serve, you need to inquire as to its investment minimums.

An excellent and typically more affordable alternative to large institutions is to select an attorney or a Certified Public Accountant (CPA) you trust and who does this type of work regularly. They are much more likely to have a relationship with you and your family, thereby understanding the specific needs and nuances of your particular blended-family scenario. Your family also is less likely impacted by the ongoing turnover that can often occur in larger institutions.

Choosing an individual who does not have a stake or conflict of interest in terms of how the money and assets are invested is also a wise move. The downside to choosing an individual is that he or she takes on all the liability and can be challenged to follow through with the specific wishes of the trust and estate plan. It is essential that you take time to describe your desires in detail so that those in governance roles can rest assured that they are well-guided toward making the best fiduciary decisions they can for you, your estate, and the various needs of your different family members, whatever their blood, legal, or love relationship to you.

Despite my strongest recommendations, most people want a family member to serve as executor or trustee. In non-blended-family situations, this can cause problems, particularly if there are hurt feelings or if the wrong family member is chosen. However, in blended families where you intend to leave your estate to both your partner and your children from a prior union, family members often have inherent conflicts of interest that make it ill-advisable for them to serve in either capacity.

Why the Surviving Partner May Have Conflicts of Interest

If you are dividing your estate between your partner and your children and you're thinking of naming your partner as executor; trustee of any testamentary trust for the joint benefit of your partner and your children; or as successor trustee of your living trust, you should immediately recognize that your partner, as an interested party, has a conflict of interest. It is merely human instinct to take care of yourself first. There are many judgment calls and elections that need to be made while administering an estate or trust, and these matters can have the effect of favoring one group of heirs or beneficiaries over another, and vice versa. It is human nature to benefit yourself over the interests of others.

Your partner is probably aware that you're doing estate planning, and he or she may express a strong desire to serve. Your partner may even exert pressure on you to allow him or her to serve. It is important to recognize that your partner's desire to serve often is borne out of anxiety and concern over his or her care after you are dead. Your partner is also probably fearful that you'll appoint one of your children who will use the position to disfavor the surviving partner.

There are many drivers to why a partner may express a strong desire to be executor or trustee, all of which are valid and important to figure out together. The more heated the conversation, the more likely there are fears, doubts, and anxiety that need to be addressed in the drafting of your estate plan—especially if you are both clear that neither of you should be in those roles solo, or at all.

After you two have discussed your worries and fears with each other, do your best to honor and acknowledge them as valid and normal. Then, take steps to allay each other's fears by appointing third parties that each of you may not fear as much as one of your children in the role of executor or trustee. Of course, there may be no one that either of you trusts to look after your interests other than yourselves; if that is the case, review all your options and see what steps you could take to allay the fears in other ways. This may be an important juncture to examine who you might consult with to learn more about your options.

Why the Children of the Deceased Partner May Have Conflicts of Interest

If either of you want to divide your estate between your partner and your children, it is not unusual for your respective children to exert pressure on you to appoint one of them as executor of your estate, trustee of a testamentary trust established in your will, or as successor trustee of your living trust.

Like the fears addressed previously of the surviving partner, this pressure could also be borne out of fear of potential differing views and mistreatment by the stepparent. There also may be fear of retaliation if the children have not been particularly kind or generous in their deeds or thoughts toward their stepparent. In some instances, their fear may be attributable to a hatred or deep distrust of your partner.

It is important to give your children a chance to express their worries, fears, and distrust and have those feelings acknowledged and understood. They'll know you are truly taking their considerations to heart; after all, whatever decision you make will have a lasting impact on their lives and who they will be interacting with after you are no longer there looking out for them.

You can then design your documents and statements of your wishes in such a way that they know their concerns are honored, even as you choose an impartial third party. If you do decide to give a governance role to one of your children, I strongly encourage you to make sure your partner knows and agrees with your decision and that there is excellent communication between him or her and the child in that role, preferably while you are alive.

When I was asked by a client about the possibility of having one of each of their children as coexecutors or trustees, I had an important perspective to share: "I've seen that situation several times and I don't care for it. Usually, the two groups don't know or trust each other, so each gets a separate lawyer, which adds to the expense. Then you've got the whole idea of creating a tiebreaker to clear up deadlocks."

Even larger than the issue of how much estate tax will be owed is the issue of whose share (i.e., estate tax apportionment) of the estate will be charged with the estate tax. The next section discusses the unique and potentially dangerous issue of estate tax apportionment in blended-family couples.

Understanding both sides of the conflict of interest in blended families is essential as you design your estate plan.

Estate Tax Apportionment Issues

You can address estate tax apportionment in your will or living trust. This is often included in the boilerplate legalese in the document, but it might be the most important provision in that document. If you don't address estate tax apportionment in your will or trust, your jurisdiction provides default estate tax apportionment rules, and you may or may not like those rules. This means that you need to describe your intentions to your estate planning attorney relative to estate tax apportionment. You can also provide for whose share is charged with the expenses of administering the estate or trust.

Suppose you decide to equally divide your taxable estate between your spouse and your own children, which is not uncommon. The problem is that the bequests to your children are taxable, but the bequest to your spouse is totally deductible. This will have the effect of significantly reducing what your children receive by at least 40 percent (the current United States federal estate tax rate) if the estate tax is charged solely to your children's shares. This will not affect the amount that your spouse will receive at all, so your attempt to equalize your estate between your spouse and your children will not be fulfilled as you wanted.

One possible solution is that you could charge your spouse's share with part of the children's estate tax, but that will reduce the marital deduction, which will increase the overall amount of estate tax owed. Suppose that a $20,000,000 estate is divided equally between the surviving spouse/stepparent and the decedent's children. The surviving spouse will receive $10,000,000 (less his or her share of the estate's administration expenses), but the children will receive only $8,250,000 because they will have the estate tax deducted from their share plus their share of administrative expenses, assuming other factors were calculated.

If the estate tax was partially charged to the share of the surviving spouse, the estate tax would increase and the amount he or she would receive would be reduced, but the share to the children would increase because of being relieved of part of the estate tax.

In blended families, it is not unusual for people to choose higher estate taxes over giving the surviving spouse more and their children less. Many estate planning attorneys will find this to be somewhat irrational and will have to be convinced that this is what you want, so you need to make sure this decision is well-thought-out and that you've explored all your options—not only will your attorney want to know your reasons, so will your family members. The estate planning attorney will probably have you specifically sign off on this to protect the attorney against a malpractice lawsuit by the heirs after you are gone.

If you can communicate effectively with your blended-family members about why this seems to be the only possible solution, there may be a possibility that you could all decide on something together. When everyone sees the potential financial cost of not getting along, they may discover other alternatives that might have them work together. This will allow the assets to stay together and all members of the family will benefit in ways you would ideally like to see. As you contemplate having everyone get together, you can get a sense for the likelihood and possibilities for all concerned.

Disclaimers

A disclaimer is a technique where a recipient of a bequest or inheritance simply and unconditionally refuses it timely and in writing, giving notice to the parties and in the way required by the law of your jurisdiction. The important thing in a valid disclaimer is that the person who is disclaiming can't direct where the disclaimed property will go, or the disclaimer will be treated as a gift by the disclaiming person. Disclaimers can be a very powerful and useful tool in estate planning, as they can be used in some circumstances to fix broken estate plans, as well as provide estate tax benefits.

The importance of disclaimers comes from being able to write your will in a way to anticipate a disclaimer by some of your heirs. For example, suppose one of your children doesn't want his or her share of your estate, and he or she would like for you to leave that share to his or her children. However, you still want to leave that share to your child, but you write your will so that if your child disclaims, that share goes to his or her children instead.

In traditional, nuclear families, it is not unusual for a spouse to leave his or her entire estate to his or her spouse, with the will written to leave the estate ultimately to the children if the partner disclaims, subject to the spouse's lifetime income rights, which can be very advantageous, estate tax wise. Talk to your estate planner about this technique.

Elections against a Will

You only need to worry about elections against a will if you are legally married. The elective share (also known as a "dower") is a share of a spouse's estate that the surviving spouse can claim if the surviving spouse doesn't receive it from his or her spouse. The amount of the elective share and what counts in the deceased spouse's estate vary depending on the jurisdiction in which you live. In most jurisdictions, spouses can waive their rights to the elective share in a marriage contract, which is why you see so many marriage contracts in subsequent marriage situations.

In blended-family marriages, I see many more elections against a will than in single marriages. The simple way to avoid elections against a will is to either have the spouse waive his or her elective share rights or to leave the surviving spouse enough to forestall a costly, lengthy, and often nasty court battle.[52]

---

[52] See Chapter 7 for more information about elections against a will.

11

Putting It All Together

Introduction

In my Introduction, I offered different scenarios that I commonly experience in my work with blended-family estate planning. What follows are detailed descriptions based on those scenarios to give you a rounded view of how to apply estate planning strategies as they relate to your specific family's needs.[53]

Yours, Mine, and Ours

Harry, sixty-two, and Marge, forty-eight, residents of Boston, are looking at updating their estate plan. Harry and Marge have one son together, Tom, age thirteen, but each has children of prior unions. Harry has two sons, Harry, Jr., thirty-seven, and Steve, thirty-five. Marge has a daughter, Anna, nineteen, who has a 4.0 in premed studies at Stanford University. Harry has been in Anna's life since she was three years old. Harry has two minor grandsons by Harry, Jr., who are the "apples of Harry's eye."

---

[53] If you find that your family's particular makeup and challenges are not sufficiently addressed in this chapter, contact me at paul@paulhoodservices.com, and I will be happy to consult with you about your specific questions.

Harry and Marge have been married for fifteen years. They have a prenuptial agreement providing for separate property, which they have religiously maintained and kept as separate. In the prenuptial agreement, Marge waived her right to an elective share. They describe their marriage as stable, but they often disagree on key issues. Other than being a little overweight, Harry is in good health and exercises regularly. Marge has survived both breast cancer and melanoma and has been cancer free for more than five years. They bring a financial statement, which reflects the following assets:

- Home (held in joint tenancy): $2,000,000 (owned free and clear)
- Vacation condos in Lake Tahoe and in Florida (owned as joint tenants): $1,000,000
- 90 percent interest in Harry's Inc. (Harry's separate property, a C corporation): $15,000,000
- Stock account (Marge's separate property): $1,000,000
- Stocks and bonds (Harry's separate property): $3,000,000
- Stocks and bonds (held as tenants in common): $2,000,000
- 401(k) (Harry's account through Harry's Inc. and Marge is the beneficiary): $1,800,000
- IRA (Marge's daughter, Anna, is the beneficiary): $150,000
- Bank account (held as tenants in common): $1,000,000
- Bank account (Harry's separate property): $1,500,000
- Bank account (Marge's separate property): $500,000
- Miscellaneous personal property (jointly owned): $250,000
- Life insurance: Harry $0; Marge $100,000, which is payable to Anna
- Debts: $0

Harry, Jr. works at Harry's Inc. and is being groomed to be the next CEO. Harry, Jr. is a 10 percent shareholder, and he received that stock as a gift from Harry, which exhausted Harry's $1,000,000 (then) US federal applicable exclusion amount. Harry wants Harry, Jr. to own all of the stock, unless Tom wants to get into the business. Harry's middle son, Steve, is a freelance writer and frustrated actor who earns very little if any money. Marge and Harry support Steve, who also lives with them (Marge says she doesn't like supporting or allowing Steve to live with them). However, Anna also lives with them when she's not at school (which Harry likes because he gets along well with Anna, so he gladly pays her tuition and other school expenses, and considered adopting her). The income of Harry and Marge consists of the following:

- Harry's salary at Harry's Inc.: $1,200,000
- Harry's interest and dividends: $225,000
- Marge's interest and dividends: $75,000
- Joint interest and dividends: $100,000

Harry prefers to live frugally, but Marge, a former interior designer, does not. Consequently, they require approximately $40,000 per month to live on. Marge has not used any of her lifetime applicable exclusion amount. The couple says that they're not particularly charitably inclined, although Marge volunteers for the American Cancer Society. However, Harry expressed an interest in giving money to charity instead of to the federal and state governments at death. Harry expresses an interest in "doing something" for his beloved grandchildren and in treating all his children equally, subject to taking care of Marge for her lifetime, although his sons don't trust Marge and want their shares free of any interest in favor of Marge.

Meanwhile, Marge is steadfast in her belief that the estate plan should favor Tom since he is young and has not yet completed his education, even if it means that Harry's boys get less. Marge also expresses significant discomfort when Harry exposes his sons' desire to receive their shares at his death, and Marge even said that would hurt her financially, which would be very unfair to her. Marge said that she is giving her entire estate to Anna and Tom equally in trust, since Harry has, in her words, "plenty." Harry's Inc. is in a significant growth spurt at present, due in large part to the new ideas of Harry, Jr., in whom Harry has great faith.

Should Harry and Marge be represented by the same estate planners? Given the disparity in both age and wealth levels, Harry and Marge should probably be represented by separate estate planners, even though they have a child together.

Will either Marge or Harry have to worry about a federal estate tax? Under the law as it exists today, if Harry dies first, absent a marital deduction election made in his estate, Harry's estate will owe substantial federal estate tax. At present, Marge's estate is on the cusp of having to worry about the federal estate tax, although if Harry dies first and his executor elects to take a QTIP marital deduction in Harry's estate, then Marge's estate will also have to worry about significant federal estate tax.

Should Harry's executor automatically make a QTIP election if Harry dies first to defer the federal estate tax? While it depends on what Harry's will says, Harry's executor should analyze the situation to see if the combined federal estate tax will be higher if the election is made and not simply make a knee-jerk QTIP election.

How should Harry take care of Marge? Harry's biggest concern about taking care of Marge is the disparity between her current opulent lifestyle and the small amount of income that she presently earns on her investments. Harry's problem is that the bulk of his income, his salary from Harry's, Inc., goes away at his death. One thing Harry could do is enter into a salary continuation agreement with Harry's, Inc., which could pay a percentage of his salary to the person of his choosing, presumably Marge if they are still married at his death, for a certain number of years (e.g., ten). Harry's estate also receives installment payments from Harry, Jr. relating to the sale of the stock in Harry's Inc. or even life insurance if Harry buys some, either owned by him personally or held in a life insurance trust with Marge as an income beneficiary if married to Harry at his death.

Harry could give his interests in the real estate (i.e., homes) to Marge if they are married when he dies so she wouldn't have to pay for housing. He could give Marge a lifetime trust income interest in the remainder of his estate in a QTIP trust, with his three sons as principal beneficiaries and successor income beneficiaries. However, Marge may still have to downscale her lifestyle.

If Harry's executor makes a QTIP election, should Marge waive her estate's right of reimbursement of the additional estate tax on her estate attributable to the QTIP election made in Harry's estate? While such a waiver is commonplace in single-marriage situations where the heirs of each estate are the same, Marge should not waive her estate's right to reimbursement, although she may carve that out from Tom's share, since both Harry and Marge are Tom's parents.

Should Marge be Harry's executor or trustee? Given the relationship between Harry's older children and Marge, Marge should not be named as Harry's executor or successor trustee if he uses a living trust instead. Harry should name an independent third party as executor or as trustee of any trusts that he establishes, save perhaps a separate trust for the benefit of Tom and Marge. If Marge is named as executor of Harry's estate or of any trust that holds Harry's stock in Harry's, Inc., she could fire Harry, Jr. since the estate is a 90 percent shareholder, which Harry would not want and would probably not be in the best interests of either Marge or Harry, Jr.

What should they do immediately with their real estate? Given that the marriage might not be as stable as they claim, they should consider severance of the joint tenancies, which would give Marge more net worth if she died before Harry. There is a possible ethical problem for the attorney; Marge is much more likely to survive Harry given that she is fourteen years younger. In fact, given their differences, it may be best for them to be represented by separate counsel. However, given that Marge has survived cancer twice, this might indicate that they are on even footing, since they really don't know who will survive.

It is important to note that by severing joint tenancies of out-of-state property, you are subjecting those properties to ancillary probate in those states. However, this can be overcome by putting the properties into an LLC. In any event, the ancillary probates tend to be relatively simple in most states.

There is quite a disparity between the net worth of Harry and Marge, so should this be addressed? There is an issue as to whether the disparity should be addressed at all, given the potential instability of the marriage. However, assuming they decide to consider multiple techniques, the first possible technique is estate equalization, but this is not a good idea for several reasons.

First, the marriage might not be that stable. Second, given that the estate tax is a flat tax now, and probably will remain so in the future, Harry should give Marge enough property to fully exhaust her federal estate tax applicable exclusion amount so it will pass estate tax free if she dies first. There really is no reason to equalize the estates for estate tax purposes, especially since Marge would give her share to her children only at the exclusion of Harry's sons. The problem is knowing what the United States estate tax applicable exclusion amount will be when Marge dies, assuming she predeceases Harry.

If the marriage ends in divorce, Harry will have given Marge property with no recourse to get it back. The second possible technique is the lifetime QTIP, which could put enough property into a trust to exhaust Marge's applicable exclusion amount were she to die first. This is far preferable to estate equalization. For starters, Harry could retain a contingent interest if Marge predeceased him. However, the lifetime QTIP is not without its problems. First, if the marriage fails, Harry cannot divest Marge of her interest, which must be for her lifetime. Second, there is no guarantee that the applicable exclusion amount in effect today will be in effect when Harry dies.

How can Harry accomplish all his goals? Harry wants to treat all three of his children equally, but he wants Harry, Jr. to get the whole business unless Tom gets involved in the company, in which case he wants the business to be divided between the two boys. At the outset, Harry could consider selling the company during his lifetime, which would probably maximize the value of the company, diversify the "elephant" asset in his estate, facilitate equalization of his estate between the three sons, and create significant liquidity, which would help pay the estate tax. However, this would not meet Harry's expressed goal of passing the family company on to his sons who are involved in the business. In effect, a sale would pull the rug out from under his oldest son, although the son would walk away with considerable wealth.

To treat his sons equally, Harry needs to make a catch-up bequest to his two presently uninvolved sons in order to make up for the lifetime gift of stock that he gave to Harry, Jr. Given Steve's lack of ability to handle his economic affairs and Tom's age, these legacies should be held in trust. Harry could accomplish his goals by having Harry, Jr. buy his shares from his estate at death pursuant to a buy-sell agreement. Such a plan could be financed, at least in part, by life insurance on Harry's life since the facts indicate that Harry seems to be reasonably insurable.

Of course, life insurance could also be used to "equalize" the shares of each of the other two sons, while passing the company to Harry, Jr. However, the problem with this plan is that it will be several years before Harry knows whether Tom will want to work in the company. Moreover, Harry may not be able to purchase enough insurance to fully equalize the legacies and give the entire company to Harry, Jr. The life insurance could be held in a life insurance trust, which would keep the policy proceeds out of Harry's estate.

How might a charitable lead trust assist in their estate plan? Given the present configuration of their assets, a charitable lead trust will probably not be a useful tool for Marge, whose estate is too small to warrant its use if she dies first. It's probably not a good fit for Harry's estate plan either. While Harry's estate is certainly large enough to warrant consideration of a charitable lead trust, there are several potential obstacles with the assets in their current configuration. The first such obstacle is that Harry hasn't indicated significant charitable intent, although he would prefer to give money to charity over paying the estate tax.

The second obstacle is the excess business holdings rule, which is a complicated US tax law that makes it difficult for a charity to own a large interest in a business for an extended period of time. The third obstacle is that if the charitable lead trust is intended to be a "zero-out estate tax" formula legacy, where is the necessary cash flow going to come from? Under the facts, 75 percent of the couple's income, represented by Harry's salary, goes away when Harry dies. Harry's Inc. is a C corporation that pays little if any dividends at present.

This would have to change radically in order for a charitable lead trust to work because it has to make the annual payments to the charity. Would converting Harry's, Inc. to an S corporation help at all? No, because a nongrantor charitable lead trust cannot hold S corporation stock. Therefore, for this to work, Harry would have to swap the stock during his lifetime for another asset such as cash or a note. Then, he could do an installment sale to Harry, Jr. or an intentionally defective grantor trust for the benefit of Harry, Jr. and even Tom.

Harry wants to do something for his grandchildren, so what could he do for them? For starters, Harry could pay for their health insurance, health-care expenses, and tuition without triggering a gift tax. Secondly, he could make gifts in trust of annual exclusion amounts ($15,000 in 2021) also without triggering the gift tax, although the trust must have a Crummey clause in it. The trust must be drafted to comply with the generation-skipping transfer tax rules, which are narrower than for regular gifts in trust, or Harry would have to file a gift tax return and allocate some of his generation-skipping transfer-tax exemption to each such transfer.

If Harry would like to further leverage that gift, the trust could purchase life insurance for the benefit of the grandchildren. In generation-skipping transfer trusts, I usually advise that an independent third party be the trustee instead of the parent. I find a vastly increased incidence of the parent of the grandchildren acting as if the grandchildren's money was really their own. Keeping the parent out of the role of trustee eliminates this temptation. Sometimes, children harbor resentment toward both their parents and their own children for being skipped.

Harry indicated he wants to provide for Anna's education in his will, as well as give her money for a wedding and a down payment on a home should he die before then. What could he do? Harry could establish a separate trust in his will for the benefit of Anna for at least $500,000 to cover those expenses. The trust could either terminate when Anna is thirty-five, at which point she'll receive the balance of the trust, or the trust could continue for her benefit with Anna as a co-trustee.

Empty Nesters

Bill and Marlene, both seventy-two, have been married for five years, each having buried their prior spouses. They do not have a prenuptial agreement, and they live in a common-law jurisdiction (i.e., not a community property jurisdiction). Each has grown children from their prior marriages who don't know each other very well. They live in Marlene's home, which she owns outright as an inheritance from her late husband. They survive on Social Security, rental income from Bill's condo, and Bill's IRA. They have the following assets:

- Home (Marlene): $200,000
- Condo (Bill): $100,000
- IRA (Bill): $750,000
- Personal property (Marlene): $10,000
- Personal property (Bill): $5,000

Bill and Marlene both want to take care of each other for life and to leave what's left to their respective children. Bill started to receive the required minimum distributions from his IRA at age seventy-one.

How should Bill and Marlene deal with their personal property? Bill and Marlene could each leave their respective personal property to their children, to take effect at their respective deaths so that their children receive the family heirlooms and mementoes.

How can Bill provide for both Marlene and his children? Bill's IRA is already being paid out pursuant to his remaining life expectancy. Bill could leave his IRA to a trust for the benefit of Marlene as lifetime income beneficiary and his children as principal beneficiaries.

What should Bill do with the remainder of his estate? Because he is receiving payouts from his IRA, his probate estate is growing by the amount of unspent payout from his IRA, and the IRA is shrinking. Bill should leave the balance of his property to the trust that is receiving the IRA payout.

What can Marlene do with her home? Marlene could leave her home to her children, or subject to Bill's life estate, Marlene could leave her home in trust for the benefit of Bill as income beneficiary and her children as principal beneficiaries, or Marlene could simply give her home to her children if she dies first, and Bill could move into his condo.

Eat, Drink, and Remarry

John, age sixty-three, marries his fourth wife, Judith, thirty-five. They've been married for less than three years. John has a thirty-seven-year-old son and some expensive alimony obligations to his first wife, including a requirement that he maintain life insurance for her.

Judith, who has been divorced twice, has two sons, eleven and eight, each with a different father, with whom she splits custody. Judith has substantially more wealth than John, but John has far greater income earning potential as a professional. John and Judith have a separate property prenuptial agreement. They are living in Judith's home, and they have the following assets:

- Stocks and bonds (Judith): $5,000,000
- Home (Judith): $500,000
- Personal property and vehicle (Judith): $50,000
- Bank account (Judith): $1,500,000
- Bank account (John): $50,000
- Life insurance (John and Judith is the beneficiary): $250,000 (cash value $0)
- Life insurance (John maintained for ex-wife): $1,000,000 (cash value $0)
- Stocks and bonds (John): $500,000
- Personal property and vehicles (John): $100,000
- Annual income (Judith): $150,000
- Annual income (John): $350,000

Should Judith or John engage in any significant lifetime estate planning in favor of each other? Given that they both have had multiple partners, I wouldn't recommend any significant lifetime planning in favor of each other. As far as other lifetime planning goes, I wouldn't recommend any lifetime estate planning for John since he doesn't have a taxable estate. Judith has a taxable estate, but her children are still very young, so whatever estate planning for their benefit would have to be in trust.

Depending on her individual relationships with her ex-husbands, one or both might make a good trustee for their child, but a nonparent ex-spouse should not be the trustee absent some compelling reasons. Judith could make annual exclusion gifts to the trust for the benefit of her children. Given her age and the current size of her estate, I wouldn't recommend too much significant lifetime estate planning for Judith.

Should John and Judith be represented by the same estate planners? Probably not because of the shortness of the relationship, the number of relationships each has had, the disparity of wealth between the two, and the fact that they don't share the same circumstances relative to the children (i.e., Judith's children are minors and John's son is older than Judith).

If John survives Judith, what should Judith do for John in her estate plan? Nothing should be done for him unless Judith dies while married to John. She could leave him a lifetime QTIP trust interest in her will or living trust. In that QTIP trust, she could include some of her stocks and bonds as well as her home, although the guardian for her minor children may need the home to raise the children. Given John's ability to earn a living (even though he is sixty-three, another factor to consider), Judith may well leave John nothing, although John may be able to make a spousal election, which would entitle John to a significant share of Judith's estate unless he waived his right in the prenuptial agreement.

Who should be the agents under their powers of attorney and/or successor trustees for John and Judith? Given the relatively short history of their relationship, perhaps John and Judith should have different people as their respective agents under their property and health-care powers of attorney. Judith also has the issues of her minor children to deal with. I could see Judith being John's agent under the property power of attorney more than John being Judith's agent under his property power of attorney. Nevertheless, both should at least be included in the consent documents that I discussed in Chapter 6 so that the health-care providers can talk to them about the other's health care even if they aren't each other's agents under the health-care power of attorney.

Brady Bunch

Mike, forty, a widower who has three sons, marries Carol, thirty-eight, a widow with three daughters. They have no joint children and don't plan to have any children together. The children are all minors who live together. Mike owns his own business, and Carol has a substantial separate estate that she inherited from her late first husband. They have a community property regime and no prenuptial agreement. They bought their home together, which Mike is paying for with his salary while Carol stays home with the children.

- Business (Mike): $500,000
- Bank account (Mike): $50,000
- Stocks and bonds (Carol): $3,000,000
- Home (Community): $250,000 (subject to $150,000 mortgage)
- Bank account (Community): $100,000
- Life insurance (Mike): $2,000,000 (0 cash value—his late wife is still the beneficiary, with the contingent beneficiary being his estate)
- Life insurance (Carol): $1,000,000 ($50,000 cash value—her children are the named beneficiaries but not in trust)

Should Carol and Mike be represented by the same estate planner? Even though there is a disparity in the relative wealth between the two, it is probably okay for them to be represented by the same estate planners.

Will either Mike's or Carol's estate have a federal estate tax problem? Using the current applicable exclusion amount as a barometer, the estates of neither Mike nor Carol will have any federal estate tax concerns.

Given the young ages of the children and that in both cases the other parent is deceased, shouldn't Carol and Mike consider adopting each other's children? This is an interesting question. Given the disparity in wealth between the two, the answer is might be no, although their relative wealth positions will no doubt change over time, particularly since Mike is young and working while Carol is staying home with the children. Therefore, I see no significant harm in each other adopting the other's children, although the survivor between them could still favor their own blood children in the estate plan.

What should Mike do about his life insurance? Given that Mike's deceased wife is still named as the beneficiary of the policy, Mike should change that immediately. Given the young ages of the children and that Carol is raising his children, Mike should make Carol a beneficiary of a substantial part, if not all, of the life insurance, although he could leave the insurance in a trust with Carol as the income beneficiary and his children as the principal beneficiaries (which would cover Carol's children too if Mike adopts them).

What should Carol do with her life insurance? Given that her children are minors, Carol should leave the policy proceeds to a trust for their benefit instead of simply letting each child have a substantial amount of money when they turn eighteen, which would be ill-advised.

What should Mike and Carol do with their respective shares of the family home? Given that they purchased the home together and that the home is community property, each should leave his or her interests in the family home to each other.

What should Carol do with the significant inheritance (which was life insurance proceeds) that she received from her late husband? Given that Mike and Carol have essentially agreed to raise each other's children and are all living together, if one predeceases the other, Carol should probably make Mike the income beneficiary of her estate, with her blood-related children being named the principal beneficiaries.

Given that the source of the wealth came from their father, it would not be unreasonable for her blood children to receive more of this property even if she adopts Mike's children, although this could, if not handled with good communication, cause a problem between the blood children and the adopted children. Absent a very compelling reason, I always recommend that blood children and adopted children be treated the same.

May-December Relationship

Franklin, eighty, a wealthy widower with three grown children in their fifties, marries twenty-six-year-old Bambi, an impecunious dance instructor who has a daughter, Dawn, seven, who she is raising alone. They have a prenuptial agreement, and Bambi waived her right to the spousal election. However, Franklin agreed to leave her, at a minimum, $100,000 for each year of their marriage and a minimum of $3,000,000 if they have a child together. They would like to have a child of their own. Franklin has done a substantial amount of lifetime estate planning and has passed significant wealth on to his children and grandchildren, and he has exhausted his lifetime applicable exclusion amount.

- Stocks and bonds (Franklin): $10,000,000
- Home (Franklin): $1,000,000
- Bank account (Franklin): $4,000,000
- IRA (Franklin): $500,000 (his children are the named beneficiaries)
- Income (Franklin): $750,000

- Debt (Franklin): 0
- Debt (Bambi): $25,000 (credit cards and student loans)
- Income (Bambi): $15,000
- Life insurance (Bambi): $50,000 (Dawn is the beneficiary)

Should Franklin and Bambi be represented by the same estate planners? Would this change if they have a child together? Given the recent marriage, the age disparity, and the wealth disparity between the two, they probably should be represented by separate estate planners, just as they (hopefully) were represented by separate counsel in their prenuptial agreement.

Even if the couple has a child together, caution dictates that they be represented by separate estate planners. It may well be, given that Bambi doesn't make much money, that Franklin will have to consent to pay for her estate planners. If so, he should do it without any control or say so over who she hires or how much it costs. If he does, he's opening himself up to a challenge.

How would Franklin go about implementing the prenuptial obligation to Bambi in his will or living trust? Given that the length of the marriage is unknown at present, the only way to do this is to use a formula bequest.

What sort of disability planning should Franklin do? Clearly, Franklin should have a solid property power of attorney and possibly even a living trust in addition to the property power of attorney. His disability planning should limit the agent's ability to rewrite his estate plan or change his IRA beneficiaries to protect both Franklin's children and Bambi. Bambi lacks the financial skills to serve as executor, trustee, or as agent under a property power of attorney. Franklin should name an independent third party as trustee and as agent under his property power of attorney. As far as whether Franklin's children would make a good trustee, it depends on their relationship with Bambi. I would suggest erring on the side of caution and naming an independent third party as fiduciary.

Who should be Franklin's agent under his health-care power of attorney? I see nothing wrong with naming Bambi as Franklin's agent under his health-care power of attorney. However, there should be coordination between the agents who hold the separate powers of attorney. In any event, Franklin should give his grown children access to his health-care providers through his consent form as discussed in Chapter 6.

Nontraditional Blended Family

Marie, forty-six, and Angela, thirty-seven, married recently, although they don't yet have a prenuptial agreement. As a single parent, Marie adopted a child, who is now eighteen. Angela, who has been divorced once, has a ten-year-old, whom she is raising alone. Marie stands to inherit a lot of money from her parents, but that could be in doubt due to her marriage. Angela has the greater income between the two, and she owns the home in which they live, although both are contributing to payment of the mortgage. Angela also has a potentially valuable piece of real estate that is situated on an exit corner of a proposed thoroughfare.

- Home (Angela): $250,000 (subject to $200,000 mortgage)
- Potential inheritance (Marie): $5,000,000
- Parcel of real estate (Angela): $50,000 (potentially worth about $1,000,000)
- 401(k) (Marie): $150,000
- 401(k) (Angela): $50,000
- Income (Angela): $100,000
- Income (Marie): $70,000
- Stocks and bonds (Marie): $100,000
- Stocks and bonds (Angela): $25,000
- Life insurance (Angela): $100,000 (her child is the beneficiary)
- Life insurance (Marie): $50,000 (her child is the beneficiary)

Should Marie and Angela be represented by the same estate planners? Even though there are some differences between the two women's situations, I don't see any major impediment to using the same estate planners. However, if they enter into a property agreement, they should be represented separately for that.

Should Angela and Marie have a property agreement? Given the separate nature of their respective estates and separate heirs, even though Marie is helping Angela with the mortgage on her home, the two probably should have a property agreement that could, among other things, describe the reimbursement method for the mortgage payments Angela will owe Marie if they separate.

What should Marie do about her potential inheritance? Even though Marie may not see inheritance from her parents, she should talk with them about what they may have planned, as it could impact what she does in her estate plan and how she does it. She doesn't have to tell them what to do for her. However, she could give them valuable input on what she has planned for her child and how they might structure an inheritance for her child if she was to either predecease her parents or disclaim some or all her share of the inheritance.

What should Angela do about that potentially valuable piece of real estate? Given that Angela's estate will likely not be subject to the federal estate tax, she should hold on to it unless someone is willing to pay fair value if the thoroughfare comes into fruition. If her estate is taxable in the future, and if the real estate's value hasn't increased much, she could transfer the opportunity to a trust for the benefit of her child.

Last Words of Advice

Introduction

A long time ago, a client of mine asked for the last advice that I would impart on my deathbed, meaning the nuggets of advice that I would consider so important that I would expend my final breaths on that advice—my "last, best" advice. I had to think about that carefully. I wouldn't have the luxury of time in which to give final advice (I'd be dying, after all). I'd only have the 2,000 or so words to spare here.

First, Involve Your Family

Involve your family directly in your estate planning decisions. Your estate and financial planning decisions have ramifications and impacts on your family and loved ones (including key employees in your company). These impacts can be financial and personal, and your decisions can and will affect their social relationships, jobs, and even health.

Consider the words of Seneca (a first century CE Roman philosopher) who said: "What madness is it for a man to starve himself to enrich his heir, and so turn a friend into an enemy! For his joy at your death will be proportioned to what you leave him."

Marcus Aurelius (Emperor of the Roman Empire in the second century CE) said: "A great estate is a great disadvantage to those who do not know how to use it, for nothing is more common than to see wealthy persons living scandalously and miserably; riches do them no service in order to virtue and happiness; it is precept and principle, not an estate, that makes a man good for something."

Niccolò Machiavelli (a 15th and 16th century Italian politician and author), in the famous work, *The Prince*: "A son can bear with equanimity the death of his father, but the loss of his inheritance will drive him to despair."

I could go on with quotes from others throughout history. The message remains the same: people will be impacted by their ancestors' estate planning more than just financially.

Since your family and loved ones are going to be changed by the results of your estate plan, why not involve them in its formulation? Even if someone is not going to get what he or she wants (or feels that he or she deserves), it is usually better for the other survivors to have everyone know your plans while you are still alive. Otherwise, a complainer might deny that this was your real intention. Or the person might accuse the survivors who fared better of plotting against him or her. The prospects for challenge or acrimony increase dramatically when bad news is sprung on people who then feel trapped and without options other than to attack.

One of the biggest problems in estate fights is that the star of the show has already departed the world's stage. The job of the litigants and the court is to ferret out, often with only indirect evidence, which is usually colored by the position or feelings of the giver of that evidence, what you really intended and whether you were of sound mind and free from undue influence when you did it.

Shouldn't Privacy Take Precedence?

Some clients are taken aback by my suggestion that they discuss their estate planning with their family and loved ones, believing that their privacy was supposed to be the most important aspect of their estate planning. Quite often, the clients' parents didn't involve them in their own estate planning process.

This oversight on their parents' part is not justification for the client to repeat the mistake. I'm not suggesting that you give your loved ones a vote in your estate planning decisions. Estate planning doesn't have to be a democracy. However, their input and understanding of your intent could be vital to the success or effectiveness of your estate plan, as well as in the relationships of your surviving loved ones. This is especially true in blended families and family businesses.

Different Tools and Techniques Have Different Effects

Estate planning techniques have differing impacts on your loved ones. There are a variety of estate planning techniques, and there are many variations and options within each technique. Each technique (and variation thereon) has differing potential results on relationships and finances of your loved ones. Be cognizant of the differences when you are evaluating these for your family.

Understanding Taxes

Be wary of techniques that some estate planners want you to implement just because they save taxes. In my opinion, too many estate planners pass up the opportunity to facilitate a family's healing or staying together by simply uniting them against a straw man enemy (known as the IRS).

Now here's a real secret: it's much harder (and more important) to create an estate plan that focuses on not negatively altering relationships than it is to, say, beat Uncle Sam out of estate taxes!

Be Careful about Buying into Panaceas

We have seen popularity waves of various estate planning techniques. Currently in vogue is the spousal limited access trust ("SLAT"), which has always been—and continues to be—a fine estate planning technique. Another trendy technique is the family limited partnership/LLC.

However, neither the SLAT nor the family partnerships/LLCs are for every family, even if they save estate taxes. Many spouses make fine business partners, but not all. Silent, dutiful, or cooperative children usually make fine partners, typically while at least one parent is alive. However, some children are not as silent, dutiful, and cooperative. This can be problematic when the parents ignore the partnership/LLC once established, which has tax and nontax risks.

Some children aren't suited to be, or don't know how to be, partners with parents or siblings. Some aren't suitable partners, period! The worst case here is a free-for-all by people who have been consigned together. The costs of untangling the financial and relationship matters (if it can be done) often are close to any tax savings achieved. Additionally, the IRS targets family entities aggressively, particularly those formed close to the time of death and funded with almost all the decedent's property.

I am not intending to be critical of the family partnership/LLC as an estate planning technique. I have assisted many in the formation of family partnerships/LLCs. However, it may well be that some estate planners have been heavy-handed in their "prescriptions" of family partnerships/LLCs without discussing the side effects or doing real analysis of persons likely to be involved.

Maslow's admonition applies here: "He who is good with a hammer begins to believe that everything is a nail."

Take Control, Get Involved, and Stay in Control

You must be in control of your estate planning process. Even though most estate plans are built to ensure client control, the sad fact is that most clients were not, will not be, or are not in control of the estate planning process. You may not have been in real control of selecting your estate planning advisors. Even if you were, you probably have had little say about the makeup of the aspects of your estate plan.

Given the complexities involved in estate planning techniques, you cannot expect to know as much about the technical ins and outs of estate planning as your estate planning advisors. That is why you hired them. However, don't you know more about yourself, your family, and your property than that advisor does? Of course, you do. Your knowledge and input are key ingredients in your estate plan. I firmly believe that if people felt like they could be in control of their estate planning, more people would do the right estate planning for them.

My experience has been that the quality and strength of a client's estate plan is directly proportional to the client's control of and true involvement in the estate planning process. Yet this seems to happen too seldom. Why? For starters, if you are like most people, you don't have a real idea of what you can truly accomplish, or indeed what you want to accomplish, in your estate planning. Your notion of your estate planning may vary significantly. There may be psychological reasons you will not tend to your estate planning. Maybe you feel that the grim reaper will not come for you for a long time. Or perhaps you are superstitious and believe that once your plan is done, you will die.

Avoid Planning Paralysis

I offer the following as another possible explanation planning paralysis. Planning paralysis is a feeling of helplessness, or a fear of feeling helpless, about the estate planning process. It is also a feeling which arises when people are dazed by the staggering number of estate planning options and decisions. We all like to be our own persons. We each want to control our own destiny.

Maybe you had (or heard about) a bad experience with an estate planning advisor. Maybe you are uncomfortable revealing personal or financial information to an estate planning advisor or to anyone else. Maybe you just do not trust advisors, or you feel intimidated by them. You might be concerned about cost or about not hurting someone's feelings. Or perhaps you just don't want to deal with uncomfortable thoughts.

I suspect the real reason that most people are slow to begin or follow through on estate planning is a fear losing control. Individuals fear the unknown, the "ride" you'll be on once you get started estate planning. I believe that people's fear of loss of control manifests itself in procrastination. Some may feel that they lack the requisite knowledge of the "bricks" of estate planning to intelligently debate, discern, and decide.

There is no question that your estate plan should be much more important to you than to your estate planning advisors. Advisors can and should only push a client so far. However, an advisor should at least draw a clear picture as to why the client has not made progress with an estate plan. Once a client understands the real reason he or she has not progressed, the client should be able to begin the process of dealing with his or her obstacles.

Most of all, don't delay, because time is of the essence—and no one knows if their time may be up soon.

Appendix

Recommended Books on Estate Planning (in Descending Order by Date of Publication)

The Complete Book of Wills, Estates & Trusts (4th Edition): Advice That Can Save You Thousands of Dollars in Legal Fees and Taxes, January 26, 2021, by Alexander A. Bove Jr. Esq. Melissa Langa Esq.

Let's Talk about Estate Planning: Conversations about Real-Life Missteps in Providing for Loved Ones (and Other Things you Didn't Know about Estate Planning), October 20, 2020, by Virginia A McArthur

Trustworthy: Enlightened Estate Planning, September 19, 2020, by Tara K. Wilson

The Art of Estate Planning, July 20, 2020, by Cheryl Chapman Henderson

The Savvy Client's Guide to Trusts: Is a Trust Right for You? (Savvy Client Series), January 5, 2018, by Mary L Barrow

Complete Family Wealth (Bloomberg), November 20, 2017 by James E. Hughes Jr. Susan E. Massenzio Keith Whitaker

Savvy Estate Planning: What You Need to Know before You Talk to the Right Lawyer, August 24, 2017, by James L. Cunningham Jr

Estate Planning for the Savvy Client: What You Need to Know before You Meet with Your Lawyer (Savvy Client Series) (Volume 1), March 17, 2017, by Mary L Barrow Esq

Estate Planning and the Modern Family: Old School Meets New School, July 10, 2016, by Peter A. Moustakis Esq.

Estate Planning (Wiley Corporate F&A), February 8, 2016, by William P. Streng

Family Trusts: A Guide for Beneficiaries, Trustees, Trust Protectors, and Trust Creators (Bloomberg), October 5, 2015, by Hartley Goldstone, James E. Hughes Jr., Keith Whitaker

Estate Planning Smarts (4th Edition): A Practical, User-Friendly, Action-Oriented Guide, April 30, 2015, by Deborah L. Jacobs Esq.

Beyond the Grave (Revised and Updated Edition): The Right Way and the Wrong Way of Leaving Money to Your Children (and Others), August 12, 2014, by Jeffery L. Condon

The Cycle of the Gift: Family Wealth and Wisdom, November 6, 2012 by Susan E. Massenzio, Keith Whitaker, James E. Hughes Jr.

Estate Planning for Blended Families: Providing for Your Spouse & Children in a Second Marriage, May 18, 2009, by Richard E. Barnes.

Values-Based Estate Planning: A Step-by-Step Approach to Wealth Transfer for Professional Advisors, April 13, 2000, by Scott C. Fithian

www.ingramcontent.com/pod-product-compliance
Lightning Source LLC
Chambersburg PA
CBHW071237070526
44583CB00017B/2229